Mindset Matters: Why Success is More Than Just Money

Ritu Negi

Published In: 2023
Also by **Ritu Negi**

Digital Marketing (Turn Your Passion Into Profession)
Unlock Affiliate Marketing
Copywriting (Write To Make Sales)

Created & Published In India
Copyright @ 2023 by Ritu Negi
Publish by Amazon KDP
Self-Publication
Author – Ritu Negi
ritunegiofficial@gmail.com

Introduction:

Overview of the book's purpose and key message.
Explanation of the importance of mindset in achieving success.
Brief discussion of how the book will be organized.

Part 1: The Power of Mindset

Part 2: Overcoming Limiting Beliefs

Part 3: Goal-Setting and Success Strategies

Part 4: Building a Success Mindset for Life

Overall, this book will focus on the importance of mindset in achieving success, and how cultivating a positive and growth-oriented mindset can lead to greater personal and professional fulfillment. The book will provide practical strategies and techniques for overcoming limiting beliefs, setting and achieving goals, and building a successful mindset for life. It will also emphasize that success is not just about money, but about achieving one's goals, making a positive impact, and living a fulfilling life.

Introduction

The purpose of "Mindset Matters: Why Success is More Than Just Money" is to provide you with an understanding of the importance of mindset in achieving success, and to offer practical strategies for developing a positive and growth-oriented mindset. The book's key message is that while money can be a motivator, it is not the only measure of success and that cultivating a success mindset involves more than just financial gain.

When you say success or think about the term success, the very first image that comes to our mind is being rich & famous but that's the major distraction in a way of getting the real success that is to be happy and doing what makes us happy.

You may want to measure your success with dollars but the real currency is happiness and most people with average mindsets will say, yeah we can buy happiness with money as well. But the enlightened being will say, you can buy accommodation, you can afford things that don't even require in the first place, and you can facilitate things for yourself but money doesn't change anything, it only exaggerates who you already are and it won't buy you health, peace, sleep, time, love, relation, and even you will agree that no matter how much great time you must be having, it won't last forever.

And, therefore, My only approach with this book for yourself and mine is that we shouldn't be approaching success for money but we should approach a mindset that makes us feel successful even when we don't have any money.

With the right mindset, we can have the ability to remain blissful even if we go through some failures in life and even if we want to make our dreams come true.

The book is designed to help you overcome limiting beliefs and negative self-talk, set and achieve goals, and build a successful mindset for life. It emphasizes the importance of persistence, resilience, and taking action, and provides advice on networking and finding mentors to support personal and professional growth.
By adopting a positive mindset and embracing growth, anyone can achieve their goals and build a life that is fulfilling and satisfying, both personally and professionally.
Mindset refers to the attitudes, beliefs, and perspectives that individuals have about themselves, others, and the world around them. In the context of achieving success, mindset plays a crucial role in determining whether individuals will be able to overcome obstacles, persist in the face of challenges, and make the most of opportunities.
A growth mindset, for example, emphasizes the belief that abilities and intelligence can be developed through effort and hard work, rather than being fixed or innate. This mindset allows individuals to embrace challenges and failures as opportunities for learning and growth, and to persist in the face of setbacks.
In contrast, a fixed mindset emphasizes the belief that abilities and intelligence are innate and unchangeable, which can lead to a fear of failure and a tendency to avoid challenges.

Research has shown that individuals with a growth mindset are more likely to achieve success in various domains, including academic achievement, athletic performance, and career success. This is because they are more likely to embrace challenges, persist in the face of setbacks, and seek out opportunities for growth and development.

Overall, the importance of mindset in achieving success lies in the fact that individuals who have a positive and growth-oriented mindset are more likely to overcome obstacles, persist in the face of challenges, and make the most of opportunities, ultimately leading to greater personal and professional fulfillment.

This book will be organized into four parts, each of which will focus on a different aspect of developing a success mindset.

Part 1: The Power of Mindset

This part will provide you with an overview of mindset and its impact on success. It will introduce the concept of a growth mindset, discuss the benefits of cultivating a positive mindset, and highlight the dangers of a fixed mindset. This section will also provide practical tips for developing a positive and growth-oriented mindset.

Part 2: Overcoming Limiting Beliefs

In this section, you will learn how to identify limiting beliefs and negative self-talk that can hold them back from achieving success. It will provide techniques for overcoming negative self-talk and changing limiting beliefs, and explain the power of visualization and affirmations in cultivating a success mindset.

Part 3: Goal-Setting and Success Strategies

This part will focus on setting and achieving goals, emphasizing the importance of persistence and resilience in the face of challenges and failures. It will also discuss the benefits of taking action and embracing failure as opportunities for learning and growth. Additionally, this section will address the value of networking and finding mentors to support personal and professional   growth.

Part 4: Building a Success Mindset for Life

The final part of the book will focus on building a success mindset for life, including cultivating a success mindset for personal growth and in relationships, achieving success in business and career, and building a legacy of success. It will provide practical advice on how to maintain a positive and growth-oriented mindset over   the   long   term.

Throughout the book, you will find real-world examples and practical exercises to help them apply the principles discussed in each section. By the end of the book, you will have a comprehensive understanding of the importance of mindset in achieving success and will be equipped with the tools and strategies to develop a positive and growth-oriented mindset for personal and professional fulfillment.

Part 1: The Power of Mindset

Chapter 1: Understanding Mindset and Its Impact on Success

You can find that some people live their lives in such a way that even though they don't have enough money & big achievements, they still seem happy and that's the definition of success for them.

We need to understand that not everybody is fortunate enough that they will get the best out of their hard work. Timings, situations, and places play very big roles in the achievement of big things in life.

So what's that one thing that makes you successful even though you don't have a name, fame, & money?

It's the mindset of a person, that keeps them going and trying the right thing with the right attitude.

You can either be successful or you can be significant - Or you can be both with the right mindset.

Therefore this chapter is all going to be about understanding a growth mindset and how to develop one for actual success in life.

The concept of a growth mindset is based on the belief that abilities and intelligence can be developed through effort, practice, and persistence. Individuals with a growth mindset see challenges as opportunities for growth and believe that their abilities can be improved through hard work and dedication.

The benefits of cultivating a positive mindset are numerous. Individuals with a growth mindset tend to be more resilient and better equipped to handle setbacks and failures. They are also more likely to embrace challenges, take risks, and pursue opportunities for growth and development. Additionally, individuals with a growth mindset tend to have a more positive outlook on life, which can improve their overall well-being and mental health.
In contrast, a fixed mindset is based on the belief that abilities and intelligence are fixed and unchangeable. Individuals with a fixed mindset tend to avoid challenges and risks, fearing failure and the possibility of being seen as incompetent. They also tend to view feedback as a threat to their self-worth, rather than an opportunity for growth and improvement.

The dangers of a fixed mindset are that it can limit an individual's potential for growth and development. It can also lead to a negative self-image and a lack of confidence in one's abilities. Individuals with a fixed mindset may become stuck in their comfort zones, avoiding challenges and missing out on opportunities for personal and professional growth.

Mindset refers to a person's general attitude, beliefs, and worldview. It can be defined as the set of beliefs and assumptions that shape how we think, feel, and behave. Our mindset influences the way we approach life and the decisions we make.
There are two main types of mindset: a fixed mindset and a growth mindset. A fixed mindset is the belief that our abilities and qualities are fixed and cannot be changed. In contrast, a growth mindset is a belief that we can develop our abilities and qualities

through hard work and dedication.

Our mindset can have a significant impact on our thoughts, feelings, and behaviors. For example, someone with a fixed mindset may avoid challenges or give up quickly when faced with obstacles because they believe that their abilities are fixed and cannot be improved. On the other hand, someone with a growth mindset may embrace challenges as opportunities to learn and grow and persist in the face of setbacks.

Our mindset also influences our emotional well-being. People with a growth mindset tend to have a more positive outlook on life and are more resilient in the face of adversity. They are more likely to seek out new experiences and opportunities for personal growth, which can contribute to their overall sense of well-being.

Our mindset shapes our attitudes, beliefs, and perspectives by influencing how we interpret and respond to the world around us. Our beliefs and attitudes are deeply rooted in our mindset, which is shaped by our past experiences, socialization, and cultural background.

Developing a growth mindset can help us to approach challenges with a positive attitude, pursue new opportunities, and achieve our goals.

Our mindset can have a significant impact on our ability to achieve success in various domains of life. A growth mindset can help us to overcome obstacles and develop the skills and abilities necessary to achieve our goals. On the other hand, a fixed mindset can limit our potential for growth and development, making it harder to achieve success.

Here are a few ways in which mindset can impact our ability to achieve success in different domains of life:

1. **Academic success:** A growth mindset can help us to approach learning with a positive attitude, seeing mistakes and failures as opportunities for learning and growth. This can lead to greater motivation and effort, which can result in better grades and academic performance.
2. **Career success:** A growth mindset can help us to develop the skills and abilities necessary to succeed in our chosen career path. By embracing challenges and seeking out new opportunities for growth and development, we can improve our performance and advance our careers.
3. **Relationships:** A growth mindset can also impact our ability to develop and maintain healthy relationships. By approaching relationships with a positive attitude, and seeing challenges and disagreements as opportunities for learning and growth, we can build stronger and more meaningful connections with others.
4. **Health and wellness:** A growth mindset can also help us to achieve success in our health and wellness goals. By approaching fitness and nutrition with a positive attitude, and seeing setbacks and challenges as opportunities to learn and grow, we can develop the habits and behaviors necessary for long-term success.

A growth mindset can help individuals embrace challenges, persist in the face of setbacks, and seek out opportunities for growth and development by promoting a positive attitude towards learning and growth, and by encouraging individuals to take risks and push themselves outside of their comfort zones. By embracing a growth mindset, individuals can achieve greater success in all areas of their lives.

Here are some ways in which this mindset can help individuals achieve these goals:

1. **Embracing challenges:** People with a growth mindset tend to see challenges as opportunities for learning and growth. They believe that their abilities can be developed through hard work and dedication. As a result, they are more likely to take on new challenges and push themselves outside of their comfort zones.
2. **Persisting in the face of setbacks:** People with a growth mindset understand that setbacks and failures are a natural part of the learning process. They see these experiences as opportunities to learn and grow, rather than as signs of personal inadequacy. As a result, they are more likely to persist in the face of obstacles and setbacks, and to use these experiences as motivation to work harder and smarter.

3. **Seeking out opportunities for growth and development:** People with a growth mindset are always looking for ways to learn and improve. They are curious and open-minded, seeking out new experiences and challenges. They are not afraid to ask for feedback or help when needed and are always looking for ways to develop new skills and abilities.

While a growth mindset can be beneficial for personal growth and development, it is not without its potential drawbacks. In some cases, individuals with a growth mindset may develop a fear of failure and a tendency to avoid challenges.

Here are some ways in which this can happen:

1. Unrealistic expectations: People with a growth mindset may set unrealistic expectations for themselves, believing that they can achieve anything if they work hard enough. When they encounter setbacks or failures, they may become discouraged and fearful of trying again, leading them to avoid challenges in the future.

2. Negative self-talk: Individuals with a growth mindset may be more likely to engage in negative self-talk when they encounter obstacles or setbacks. They may view these experiences as evidence of personal inadequacy or failure, leading them to feel discouraged and fearful of trying again.

3. Overemphasis on achievement: People with a growth mindset may place too much emphasis on achievement and success, viewing failure as a personal failure rather than as a natural part of the learning process. This can lead to a fear of failure and a tendency to avoid challenges that may be perceived as too risky or uncertain.

4. Lack of support: Individuals with a growth mindset may be less likely to seek out support from others when they encounter challenges or setbacks. This can lead to feelings of isolation and discouragement, which can exacerbate their fear of failure and tendency to avoid challenges.

A growth mindset can lead to a fear of failure and a tendency to avoid challenges when individuals set unrealistic expectations, engage in negative self-talk, overemphasize achievement, or lack support. To avoid these potential drawbacks, it is important for individuals to maintain a balanced perspective on their abilities and achievements, to seek out support from others when needed, and to view failure as a natural part of the learning process.

There are many examples of individuals who have adopted a growth mindset and achieved success in various domains of life. Here are a few real-world examples:

1. **Michael Jordan:** Considered one of the greatest basketball players of all time, Michael Jordan is a prime example of someone who has embraced a growth mindset. Despite being cut from his high school basketball team, Jordan worked hard to develop his skills and went on to win six NBA championships and numerous awards throughout his career.

2. **Oprah Winfrey:** Oprah Winfrey is a media mogul who has built an empire on the principles of growth and personal development. Despite a challenging childhood and early setbacks in her career, Winfrey remained committed to learning and growing, eventually becoming one of the most influential and successful women in the world.

3. **Thomas Edison:** Inventor Thomas Edison is known for his many innovations, including the light bulb and the phonograph. Despite encountering numerous setbacks and failures throughout his career, Edison remained committed to his work and saw each setback as an opportunity to learn and grow.

4. **J.K. Rowling:** Best-selling author J.K. Rowling is another example of someone who has embraced a growth mindset. After being rejected by multiple publishers, Rowling continued to work on her writing and eventually published the first Harry Potter book, which went on to become a global phenomenon.

5. **Elon Musk:** Entrepreneur Elon Musk has achieved success in multiple domains, including the automotive, aerospace, and energy industries. Despite numerous setbacks and failures throughout his career, Musk remains committed to innovation and growth, continually pushing himself and his companies to achieve greater success.

In each of these examples, the individuals have demonstrated a commitment to learning, growth, and personal development. By embracing a growth mindset, they have been able to overcome obstacles, persist in the face of setbacks, and achieve success in various domains of life.

Here are some practical tips for developing a positive and growth-oriented mindset:

Practice positive self-talk: Pay attention to your inner dialogue and replace negative self-talk with positive affirmations. Instead of saying "I can't do this," say "I can do this with effort and practice." This can help you cultivate a growth mindset and build self-confidence.

Visualize success: Visualize yourself achieving your goals and overcoming challenges. This can help you build a positive mindset and develop a sense of resilience when faced with setbacks.

Set realistic goals: Set goals that are challenging but achievable. This can help you build a sense of momentum and accomplishment, which can reinforce a positive and growth-oriented mindset.

Embrace failure as an opportunity for growth: Don't view failure as a personal failure but as a learning experience. Analyze what went wrong and what you can do differently next time. This can help you develop a growth mindset and build resilience.

Practice gratitude: Cultivate a sense of gratitude for what you have, rather than focusing on what you lack. This can help you maintain a positive mindset and develop a sense of resilience in the face of challenges.

Use positive affirmations: Use positive affirmations to reinforce your positive mindset. Affirmations like "I am capable of achieving my goals" or "I am resilient and can overcome obstacles" can help you stay motivated and positive.

Surround yourself with positive influences: Surround yourself with positive people who support your goals and aspirations. This can help you maintain a positive and growth-oriented mindset.

Developing a positive and growth-oriented mindset involves practicing positive self-talk, visualization, affirmations, setting realistic goals, embracing failure as an opportunity for growth, practicing gratitude, and surrounding yourself with positive influences. By adopting these practices, you can cultivate a positive and growth-oriented mindset and achieve success in various domains of life.

Here are some tools and strategies that can help you develop a positive and growth-oriented mindset for personal and professional fulfillment:

1. **Mindfulness:** Mindfulness practices, such as meditation and deep breathing, can help you become more aware of

your thoughts and emotions, which can help you identify and challenge negative thinking patterns.

2. **Journaling:** Journaling can help you process your thoughts and emotions and gain clarity on your goals and aspirations. It can also help you identify limiting beliefs and develop a more positive and growth-oriented mindset.

3. **Learning new skills:** Learning new skills and taking on new challenges can help you build confidence and develop a growth-oriented mindset. It can also help you develop a sense of resilience and adaptability.

4. **Seeking out feedback:** Seeking feedback from others can help you identify areas for growth and improvement. It can also help you develop a more growth-oriented mindset by seeing feedback as an opportunity for learning and growth.

5. **Practicing self-compassion:** Practicing self-compassion can help you develop a more positive and growth-oriented mindset by acknowledging and accepting your imperfections and mistakes. It can also help you develop a sense of resilience in the face of setbacks.

6. **Setting meaningful goals:** Setting meaningful goals can help you develop a growth-oriented mindset by giving you something to work towards and providing a sense of purpose and direction.

7. **Cultivating a growth mindset community:** Surrounding yourself with others who share a growth mindset can help you stay motivated and inspired. This can be done by joining communities, attending events, or finding like-

minded individuals online.

Developing a positive and growth-oriented mindset requires intentional effort and the implementation of specific tools and strategies. By practicing mindfulness, journaling, learning new skills, seeking feedback, practicing self-compassion, setting meaningful goals, and cultivating a growth mindset community, you can develop a positive and growth-oriented mindset that will contribute to both personal and professional fulfillment.

Chapter 2: The Benefits of a Growth Mindset

A growth mindset refers to the belief that abilities and talents can be developed through hard work, dedication, and perseverance. The concept of a growth mindset was popularized by psychologist Carol Dweck, who found that individuals with a growth mindset were more likely to embrace challenges and persist in the face of obstacles.
One with a growth mindset lives a certain lifestyle that includes the bigger picture of developing small habits.

People with a growth mindset believe in the compound effects of highly successful habits in day-to-day life. They don't work for small & instant achievements, they understand the value of patience & persistence and one with this mindset can never get insecure about their life and that's the real success in life, doing what is needed over on what is desirable.

Here are some key points on the benefits of a growth mindset

Increased motivation: When you have a growth mindset, you believe that your abilities can improve with effort and practice. This belief can lead to greater motivation to learn and develop new skills. Having a growth mindset can lead to increased motivation because it helps you believe that your efforts and actions can lead to positive outcomes. When you believe that you can improve and develop new skills, you are more likely to be motivated to put in the necessary work and effort to achieve your goals.

increased motivation can lead to a more positive outlook and a greater sense of control over one's life. This can lead to increased confidence, better mental health, and overall success in various areas of life. Thus, having a growth mindset and increasing one's motivation can be a crucial components in achieving success and personal fulfillment.

There was a young woman named Sarah who had always struggled with math. She had been told by her teachers and peers that she just wasn't good at it, and she began to believe that her abilities were fixed and unchangeable.

But one day, Sarah decided to challenge herself and take an advanced math course. At first, she struggled and felt discouraged, but she was determined to succeed. She began to approach the subject with a growth mindset, believing that she could improve with effort and practice.

Sarah sought out extra help, practiced problems every day, and took risks by participating in class discussions. She slowly but steadily began to improve, and her confidence grew with each passing day.

As her grades began to improve, Sarah's motivation also increased. She was excited to see the progress she was making and felt a renewed sense of purpose and determination. She even began to consider pursuing a career in a math-related field.

In the end, Sarah's growth mindset not only helped her succeed in math but also had a positive impact on other areas of her life. She became more confident, persistent, and motivated, leading to success and personal fulfillment.

Sarah's story is a testament to the power of a growth mindset and the positive impact it can have on one's life. When we believe that we can improve and develop new skills, we are more likely to be motivated to put in the necessary effort and achieve our goals.

Greater creativity and innovation: A growth mindset encourages you to think outside the box and explore new possibilities. This can lead to greater creativity and innovation in your work and personal life.

A growth mindset can lead to greater creativity and innovation because it encourages individuals to approach problems and challenges with an open mind and a willingness to try new things. When you believe that your abilities can improve with effort and practice, you are more likely to be open to new ideas and take risks.

Here are some ways in which a growth mindset can foster greater creativity and innovation:

mbracing failure: Individuals with a growth mindset see failure as an opportunity for learning and growth. This mindset allows them to take risks and try new things without fear of failure, which can lead to more creative and innovative ideas.
1. **Challenging assumptions:** A growth mindset encourages individuals to challenge their own assumptions and biases. By questioning assumptions and looking at problems from different perspectives, individuals can come up with more creative and innovative solutions.
2. **Seeking out new experiences:** Individuals with a growth mindset are more likely to seek out new experiences and

challenges. This can lead to exposure to new ideas and perspectives, which can spark creativity and innovation.

3. **Collaborating with others:** Individuals with a growth mindset are often more open to collaborating with others and learning from their perspectives. This can lead to more diverse and innovative ideas.

A growth mindset encourages individuals to be more open-minded and flexible, which can lead to greater creativity and innovation. By embracing challenges and being willing to try new things, individuals can break out of their comfort zones and come up with new and innovative solutions to problems.

Improved problem-solving skills: A growth mindset can help you approach problems with a more positive and constructive attitude. Instead of becoming discouraged or giving up when faced with a challenge, you are more likely to persist and find a solution.

A growth mindset can lead to improved problem-solving skills because it fosters a positive attitude toward challenges and encourages individuals to approach problems with a flexible and open-minded perspective.

Individuals with a growth mindset view challenges as opportunities for growth and learning, rather than as obstacles. This mindset helps individuals to approach problems with a positive attitude, which can lead to improved problem-solving skills. It encourages individuals to persist in the face of obstacles and setbacks. This persistence can help individuals to overcome difficult problems and find creative solutions.

Individuals with a growth mindset are more likely to be open to different approaches and perspectives. This flexibility allows them to consider different solutions to problems and to adapt their approach as needed. A growth mindset encourages individuals to view mistakes as opportunities for learning. By analyzing mistakes and understanding what went wrong, individuals can improve their problem-solving skills for the future.

Individuals with a growth mindset are more likely to seek out feedback and input from others. This can help individuals to gain new perspectives and insights, leading to improved problem-solving skills.

A growth mindset can improve problem-solving skills by encouraging individuals to approach challenges with a positive attitude, persistence, flexibility, and a willingness to learn and seek feedback.

Increased resilience: One of the most important benefits of a growth mindset is increased resilience. When you believe that you can improve and grow, setbacks and failures are seen as opportunities to learn and improve, rather than as evidence of a fixed ability or personal deficiency. Resilience is the ability to bounce back from adversity and to adapt to change, and a better mindset can help individuals to develop this ability.

Once there was a young woman named Maya who dreamed of becoming a successful entrepreneur. She worked hard to build her business from scratch but faced many challenges along the way. She encountered setbacks, rejections, and even financial struggles.

Despite these difficulties, Maya maintained a growth mindset. She believed that with hard work, perseverance, and a willingness to learn, she could overcome any obstacle. She focused on her strengths and used her failures as opportunities for growth.

One day, Maya's business hit a major roadblock. A key partnership fell through, leaving her feeling defeated and unsure of what to do next. But instead of giving up, Maya took a step back and reflected on her options. She brainstormed new ideas, sought feedback from mentors, and stayed positive even in the face of uncertainty.

Through her resilience and determination, Maya was able to pivot her business in a new direction and ultimately achieve even greater success than she had imagined. Her growth mindset allowed her to bounce back from setbacks and persevere through challenges, ultimately leading her to achieve her dreams.

Maya's story shows that with a growth mindset, we can cultivate resilience in the face of adversity. By embracing challenges, staying flexible, and focusing on our strengths, we can overcome obstacles and achieve our goals.

Overall, cultivating a growth mindset can lead to greater success and fulfillment in all areas of life. By embracing challenges, learning from mistakes, and persisting in the face of obstacles, individuals with a growth mindset are better equipped to achieve their goals and reach their full potential.

Chapter 3: The Dangers of a Fixed Mindset

In life, we all face challenges and setbacks that can test our resolve and challenge our beliefs about ourselves and our abilities. For some of us, these challenges can lead to a growth mindset, in which we see opportunities for learning and growth in every obstacle we encounter. But for others, these challenges can trigger a fixed mindset, in which we believe that our abilities and qualities are fixed and cannot be changed.

In this chapter, we will explore the dangers of a fixed mindset and the ways in which it can hold us back in our personal and professional lives. We will examine the negative beliefs and behaviors that are associated with a fixed mindset, including a fear of failure, a lack of motivation, resistance to change, and negative self-talk.

We will also discuss the ways in which a fixed mindset can limit our potential and prevent us from achieving our goals. By understanding the dangers of a fixed mindset and the ways in which it can hold us back, we can begin to cultivate a growth mindset and unlock our full potential for success and personal growth.

Fear of failure

Individuals with a fixed mindset are more likely to fear failure because they believe that their abilities are fixed and cannot be changed. This fear of failure can prevent individuals from taking risks, trying new things, and pursuing their goals.

A fixed mindset can lead to a fear of failure because individuals with this mindset believe that their abilities and qualities are fixed and cannot be changed. This means that they view failure as a reflection of their inherent flaws or shortcomings, rather than as an opportunity for growth and learning.

For example, let's say that someone with a fixed mindset wants to learn a new skill, such as playing the guitar. They may believe that they either have a natural talent for music or they don't and that there's nothing they can do to improve their skills if they don't have that innate talent.
This belief can lead to a fear of failure, as they may be hesitant to even attempt to learn the skill for fear of not being naturally good at it. If they do attempt to learn the skill and encounter difficulty, they may become discouraged and give up easily, rather than persevering and using their failures as opportunities for growth.

A fixed mindset can lead to a fear of failure because it limits our belief in our ability to improve and grow. By cultivating a growth mindset and embracing challenges as opportunities for growth, we can overcome our fear of failure and unlock our full potential for success and personal growth.

Fear of failure can be dangerous because it can limit our ability to take risks, pursue our goals, and reach our full potential.

Firstly, fear of failure can prevent us from taking risks and trying new things. When we are afraid of failure, we may avoid challenges or opportunities that could lead to personal and professional growth. This can limit our ability to learn, develop new skills, and achieve our goals.

Secondly, fear of failure can lead to procrastination and indecisiveness. When we are afraid of failure, we may spend too much time thinking about the potential consequences of our actions, rather than taking action. This can lead to a lack of progress and missed opportunities.

Thirdly, fear of failure can contribute to low self-esteem and self-doubt. When we are afraid of failure, we may begin to doubt our abilities and our worth as individuals. This can lead to negative self-talk and a lack of self-confidence, which can further limit our ability to pursue our goals and achieve success.

Overall, fear of failure can be dangerous because it can limit our ability to take risks, learn, and grow. By cultivating a growth mindset and embracing challenges as opportunities for learning and growth, we can overcome our fear of failure and reach our full potential for success and personal development.

Lack of motivation

A fixed mindset can lead to a lack of motivation because individuals with this mindset believe that their abilities and qualities are fixed and cannot be changed. This means that they may believe that their efforts won't make a difference in their outcomes, and as a result, they may feel helpless and lack the motivation to pursue their goals.

For example, let's say that someone with a fixed mindset wants to apply for a job that requires a certain set of skills. However, they believe that these skills are innate and cannot be developed through practice or learning. As a result, they may feel discouraged from applying for the job because they do not believe that their efforts to learn the skills will make a difference in their chances of success.

Similarly, someone with a fixed mindset may avoid challenges or difficult tasks because they believe that they will not be able to improve their abilities or overcome the obstacles. This can lead to a lack of motivation to pursue goals that require effort, perseverance, and hard work.

In contrast, someone with a growth mindset would view their efforts as valuable and necessary for their growth and development. They would embrace challenges and difficulties as opportunities to learn and improve their skills, and they would be motivated by the possibility of achieving their goals through their hard work and dedication.

A fixed mindset can lead to a lack of motivation because it limits our belief in our ability to improve and grow. By cultivating a growth mindset and embracing challenges as opportunities for growth, we can overcome our lack of motivation and unlock our full potential for success and personal growth.

Resistance to change

A fixed mindset can lead to resistance to change because individuals with this mindset believe that their abilities and qualities are fixed and cannot be changed. This means that they may feel threatened by new experiences, challenges, or feedback that could challenge their existing beliefs and abilities.

Resistance to change can be dangerous because it can prevent us from adapting to new circumstances and opportunities for growth. When we resist change, we may miss out on important opportunities to learn, grow, and succeed.

For example, let's say that an organization is implementing a new technology system to streamline its operations. However, some employees are resistant to the change because they are comfortable with the old system and fear that they may not be able to learn the new system. This resistance can lead to decreased productivity, delays in implementing the new system, and missed opportunities for efficiency and growth.
Similarly, in our personal lives, resistance to change can prevent us from pursuing new opportunities, learning new skills, or overcoming challenges. It can limit our ability to grow and develop as individuals and can lead to missed opportunities for personal and professional success.

Moreover, resistance to change can create stress, anxiety, and frustration, which can have negative effects on our mental and physical well-being. It can also create tension and conflict in our relationships, both personal and professional.

Overall, resistance to change can be dangerous because it can limit our ability to adapt to new circumstances, learn and grow, and achieve our goals. By cultivating a growth mindset and embracing new experiences and challenges as opportunities for growth, we can overcome our resistance to change and unlock our full potential for success and personal growth.

Negative self-talk

A fixed mindset can lead to negative self-talk, in which individuals criticize themselves for their perceived shortcomings and failures. This negative self-talk can lead to low self-esteem, self-doubt, and a lack of confidence.

A fixed mindset can lead to negative self-talk because individuals with this mindset tend to believe that their abilities and qualities are fixed and cannot be changed. This means that when they encounter challenges or setbacks, they may interpret these experiences as evidence of their fixed limitations or shortcomings.

For example, let's say that someone with a fixed mindset struggles to learn a new skill or subject. They may interpret this struggle as evidence that they are not smart enough or talented enough to succeed in that area. This negative self-talk can then create a self-fulfilling prophecy, leading them to avoid or give up on that skill or subject, which in turn reinforces their fixed mindset and negative self-talk.

Similarly, someone with a fixed mindset may engage in negative self-talk when they experience failure or setbacks. They may interpret these experiences as evidence of their fixed limitations, rather than as opportunities for growth and learning. This negative self-talk can then create feelings of hopelessness, which can further reinforce their fixed mindset and limit their ability to learn and grow.
Negative self-talk can be dangerous because it can lead to a number of negative outcomes for our mental and physical well-being, as well as for our personal and professional success.

Firstly, negative self-talk can contribute to feelings of anxiety, stress, and depression. When we engage in negative self-talk, we are essentially reinforcing negative beliefs about ourselves, which can lead to feelings of hopelessness and helplessness. Over time, these negative emotions can have a negative impact on our mental and physical health.

Secondly, negative self-talk can lead to a lack of motivation and self-confidence. When we constantly criticize ourselves and focus on our weaknesses, we may begin to doubt our ability to succeed and achieve our goals. This lack of motivation and self-confidence can then limit our ability to pursue new opportunities and reach our full potential.

Thirdly, negative self-talk can lead to self-sabotage. When we engage in negative self-talk, we may begin to believe that we are not capable of succeeding, which can lead us to avoid or give up on opportunities for growth and success. This can limit our personal and professional success and prevent us from reaching our goals.

Overall, negative self-talk can be dangerous because it can limit our ability to succeed and achieve our goals, and can have negative impacts on our mental and physical well-being. By cultivating a growth mindset and engaging in positive self-talk, we can overcome our negative beliefs and unlock our full potential for success and personal growth. The chapter emphasizes that a fixed mindset can be a major obstacle to success and personal growth. By recognizing the dangers of a fixed mindset and cultivating a growth mindset instead, individuals can unlock their full potential and achieve greater success in all areas of their lives.

Chapter 4: How to Develop a Positive Mindset

Developing a positive mindset is not an easy task, but it is a journey that can lead to a happier, more fulfilled life.
This chapter offers you practical tips and strategies for cultivating a positive and growth-oriented mindset. These tips include focusing on gratitude, reframing negative thoughts, surrounding oneself with positivity, embracing failure, and taking care of physical and mental health.

Each tip is explained in detail and accompanied by practical strategies that you can apply in your daily life to develop a more positive mindset. By providing actionable steps, the chapter empowers you to take control of your mindset and cultivate a more positive outlook, which can lead to greater success, resilience, and happiness.

Developing a positive mindset can improve both your mental and physical health, increase resilience, and improve relationships and productivity. By cultivating a positive mindset, you can lead a happier, more fulfilling life.

Developing a positive mindset is important for several reasons:

Improved mental health: A positive mindset can improve mental health by reducing stress, anxiety, and depression. By focusing on the positive aspects of life, you can reduce negative thoughts and improve your overall well-being.

Increased resilience: A positive mindset can help you bounce back from setbacks and challenges. When you face obstacles, a positive mindset can help you stay optimistic and motivated to overcome them.

Improved relationships: A positive mindset can also improve your relationships with others. When you have a positive attitude, you are more likely to be kind, compassionate, and understanding toward others.

Increased motivation: A positive mindset can also increase your motivation and productivity. When you focus on the positive aspects of your goals, you are more likely to be motivated to achieve them.

Improved physical health: Research has shown that a positive mindset can improve physical health by reducing stress, improving immune function, and promoting healthy behaviors.

Mindset not only enhances personal and professional life but it's the most required element to live a peaceful life. With an unstable mindset, you can get insecure very easily by watching other people grow whereas a person with the right mindset will appreciate and learn from others' success as well. And that's why it's very important to develop a positive mindset because success is more than just money.

Here are some steps to develop a positive mindset:

Reframing negative thoughts

Reframing negative thoughts is an important step in developing a positive mindset. When we have negative thoughts, it can impact our emotions, behaviors, and overall outlook on life. Reframing these thoughts involves changing the way we think about a situation or event, which can shift our mindset towards a more positive perspective.

Instead of seeing challenges as obstacles, try to reframe them as opportunities to learn and grow. This shift in perspective can help you approach difficult situations with a positive and growth-oriented mindset.
Negative thoughts can cause stress and anxiety, which can impact our physical and mental health. By reframing negative thoughts into more positive ones, we can reduce the stress and anxiety we feel.

When we have a negative mindset, we may feel stuck or unable to find solutions to problems. Reframing negative thoughts can help us approach problems with a more positive and solution-focused mindset, improving our problem-solving skills.

Negative thoughts can undermine our self-esteem and confidence. By reframing negative thoughts into more positive ones, we can improve our self-esteem and feel more confident in ourselves and our abilities.

Reframing negative thoughts can help us build resilience and bounce back from setbacks and challenges. By focusing on the positive aspects of a situation, we can stay optimistic and motivated to overcome obstacles.

Reframing negative thoughts is a powerful tool in developing a positive mindset. By changing the way we think about situations and events, we can reduce stress, improve problem-solving skills, enhance self-esteem, and build resilience.

Reframing negative thoughts can be challenging, but it is an important step in developing a positive mindset. Here are some strategies for reframing negative thoughts:

Identify the negative thought: The first step in reframing negative thoughts is to identify them. Notice when you are having negative thoughts and write them down.

Challenge the negative thought: Once you have identified the negative thought, challenge it. Ask yourself if the thought is really true or if there is evidence to support it.

Find evidence to support a positive thought: Look for evidence to support a positive thought. For example, if you are thinking "I am not good enough," look for evidence that contradicts this thought, such as past accomplishments or positive feedback from others.

Reframe the negative thought into a positive one: Once you have found evidence to support a positive thought, reframe the negative thought into a positive one. For example, "I am not good enough" can become "I am capable and have accomplished many things in the past."

Practice positive self-talk: Once you have reframed negative thoughts into positive ones, practice positive self-talk. Repeat positive affirmations to yourself, such as "I am capable" or "I can handle this."

Reframing negative thoughts takes practice, but over time, it can help shift your mindset towards a more positive outlook. By challenging negative thoughts and finding evidence to support positive ones, you can develop a positive mindset that can lead to greater success and happiness.

Practicing gratitude

Focusing on the positive things in your life can help you develop a more positive outlook. The chapter recommends keeping a gratitude journal and regularly reflecting on the things you are grateful for.

Practicing gratitude is an important aspect of developing a positive mindset. Gratitude is the practice of focusing on the good in our lives, rather than the negative. Here are some ways practicing gratitude can help in developing a positive mindset:

1. **Increases positivity:** When we practice gratitude, we focus on the positive aspects of our lives. This can help increase our overall positivity and improve our outlook on life.
2. **Reduces stress:** Focusing on gratitude can also help reduce stress. When we feel grateful, it can shift our focus away from negative thoughts and emotions, which can lower stress levels.
3. **Improves relationships:** Practicing gratitude can also improve our relationships with others. When we express gratitude to others, it can strengthen our connections and improve our social support.
4. **Enhances well-being:** Gratitude has been linked to improved mental and physical health. By focusing on the good in our lives, we can enhance our overall well-being.

Here are some ways to practice gratitude:

1.Keep a gratitude journal: Write down things you are grateful for each day. This can help you focus on the positive aspects of your life.

2. Express gratitude to others: Thank others for the positive impact they have had on your life. This can improve your relationships and enhance your social support.

3. Focus on the present moment: When you are present in the moment, you can appreciate the good in your life. Try to focus on the present moment and notice the good around you.

Overall, practicing gratitude is an effective way to develop a positive mindset. By focusing on the good in our lives, we can increase positivity, reduce stress, improve relationships, and enhance well-being.

Surrounding yourself with positive influences

The people we surround ourselves with can have a significant impact on our mindset. The chapter suggests seeking out positive and supportive people who will encourage and motivate you. Surrounding yourself with positive influences is important for developing a positive mindset for several reasons:

Positive influences can inspire and motivate you. When you surround yourself with positive people, you are more likely to be inspired and motivated by their positive attitudes and actions. This can help you maintain a positive mindset and stay focused on your goals.

Negative influences can drain your energy. Conversely, when you surround yourself with negative influences, they can drain your energy and bring you down. This can make it harder to maintain a positive mindset and achieve your goals.

Positive influences can provide support. When you surround yourself with positive people, you are more likely to receive support and encouragement. This can help you stay motivated and overcome challenges.

Positive influences can provide perspective. Positive influences can also provide perspective and help you see the positive aspects of a situation. This can help you maintain a positive mindset even in challenging times.

Positive influences can help you grow. When you surround yourself with positive influences, you are more likely to grow and develop as a person. Positive people can provide feedback and guidance, and challenge you to be your best self.

Overall, surrounding yourself with positive influences is essential for developing a positive mindset. Positive influences can inspire and motivate you, provide support and perspective, and help you grow as a person.

Taking care of your physical and mental health

Our physical and mental health can have a significant impact on our mindset. The chapter recommends prioritizing self-care activities such as exercise, meditation, and getting enough sleep. Taking care of your physical and mental health is essential for developing a positive mindset. It can help improve your mood, increase your energy, reduce stress, increase self-confidence, and boost resilience. By prioritizing your health, you can create a foundation for a positive and fulfilling life.

Taking care of your physical and mental health can help improve your mood. Exercise and other physical activities release endorphins, which are known to improve mood and reduce stress. Taking care of your mental health by engaging in self-care practices like meditation, therapy, or spending time with loved ones can also help improve your mood.

When you take care of your physical health by eating a balanced diet, getting enough sleep, and exercising regularly, you can increase your energy levels. Having more energy can help you stay focused and motivated, and can contribute to a more positive mindset.

Taking care of your mental health can help reduce stress. Engaging in stress-reducing activities like mindfulness, deep breathing, or journaling can help calm your mind and reduce stress levels.

Taking care of your physical health can increase your self-confidence. When you take care of your body, you feel better about yourself and your abilities. This can help you feel more positive and optimistic about your life.

Taking care of your physical and mental health can help increase your resilience. When you are physically and mentally healthy, you are better equipped to handle challenges and setbacks, which can help you maintain a positive mindset.

Taking care of your physical and mental health can involve a range of activities and practices. Here are some strategies you can use:

1. **Exercise regularly:** Engage in regular physical activity to improve your physical health and release endorphins that can boost your mood.

2. **Eat a balanced diet:** A healthy diet can provide the nutrients your body needs to function properly and support your mental health.

3. **Get enough sleep:** Adequate sleep is essential for maintaining physical and mental health. Aim for 7-8 hours of sleep per night.
4. **Practice stress-reducing activities:** Activities like meditation, yoga, deep breathing, or spending time in nature can help reduce stress and improve mental health.

5. **Connect with loved ones:** Spending time with loved ones can help improve mental health and provide social support.

6. **Seek professional help:** If you are struggling with mental health issues, seek help from a mental health professional. This may involve therapy, medication, or other treatments.

7. **Take breaks:** Taking regular breaks from work or other responsibilities can help reduce stress and improve productivity.

8.. Practice self-care: Engage in activities that you enjoy and that help you relax and recharge. This might include hobbies, reading, or listening to music.

Overall, taking care of your physical and mental health requires a holistic approach that addresses your body and mind. By prioritizing your health, you can improve your mood, reduce stress, and build a foundation for a positive mindset.

Embracing failure

Failure is a natural part of the learning and growth process. The chapter encourages you to embrace failure as an opportunity to learn and grow, rather than as a personal failure.
Embracing failure is important to develop a positive mindset because it encourages growth, reduces fear, builds resilience, fosters creativity, and reduces stress. By reframing failure as an

opportunity to learn and grow, you can cultivate a more positive and optimistic outlook on life.

When you embrace failure, you view it as an opportunity to learn and grow. This encourages a growth mindset, which is focused on learning and improvement rather than fixed abilities.

When you embrace failure, you become less afraid of it. This can help you take risks and try new things, which can lead to greater success in the long run.
Embracing failure can help build resilience, which is the ability to bounce back from setbacks. By learning from failure and moving on, you can develop the ability to handle challenges and setbacks more effectively.
When you embrace failure, you become more open to new ideas and approaches. This can foster creativity and innovation, which can lead to new opportunities and successes.

When you embrace failure, you reduce stress by letting go of the pressure to be perfect. This can help you feel more relaxed and positive, which can contribute to a more positive mindset overall.

Here are some ways to embrace failure and develop a positive mindset:

1. **Reframe failure as an opportunity:** Instead of viewing failure as a negative experience, try to reframe it as an opportunity to learn and grow. Ask yourself what you can learn from the experience and how you can use it to improve in the future.

2. **Focus on effort rather than outcome:** Instead of solely focusing on the end result, try to focus on the effort you put in. Even if the outcome was not what you hoped for, if you

put in your best effort, that is a success in itself.

3. **Practice self-compassion:** Be kind to yourself when you experience failure. Treat yourself as you would a friend or loved one who is going through a tough time. This can help you maintain a positive mindset and avoid getting stuck in negative self-talk.

4. **Take action:** Instead of dwelling on your failures, take action to improve. This might involve seeking feedback, practicing new skills, or setting new goals.

5. **Embrace the process:** Instead of solely focusing on the end result, try to enjoy the process of learning and growing. Celebrate small successes along the way and enjoy the journey.

6. **Surround yourself with supportive people:** Surrounding yourself with people who encourage and support you can help you maintain a positive mindset, even in the face of failure.

Overall, embracing failure is about shifting your mindset from a fixed mindset to a growth mindset. By reframing failure as an opportunity to learn and grow, focusing on effort, practicing self-compassion, taking action, embracing the process, and surrounding yourself with supportive people, you can develop a positive mindset that helps you thrive.

In conclusion, developing a positive mindset is essential for achieving success and happiness in life. By reframing negative thoughts and focusing on the positive, you can cultivate a more optimistic outlook on life. By practicing gratitude, you can develop a greater sense of appreciation and contentment. By surrounding yourself with positive influences and taking care of your physical and mental health, you can create an environment that supports your growth and development.

Embracing failure is also an important aspect of developing a positive mindset. By reframing failure as an opportunity to learn and grow, you can develop resilience, creativity, and a growth mindset.

Overall, developing a positive mindset takes time and effort, but the benefits are worth it. By adopting these strategies and committing to a positive outlook, you can unlock your full potential and achieve success in all areas of your life.

Part 2: Overcoming Limiting Beliefs

Chapter 5: Identifying Limiting Beliefs and Negative Self-Talk

In this chapter, we will explore how our beliefs and self-talk can act as mental barriers that prevent us from achieving our full potential. We will discuss **the impact of limiting beliefs and negative self-talk on our thoughts, emotions, and behaviors, and provide practical strategies to help identify and overcome them.**

By the end of this chapter, you will have a better understanding of **how to recognize your limiting beliefs and negative self-talk,** and learn **how to reframe them into positive, empowering thoughts that support personal growth and success.** We will also discuss the importance of cultivating a growth mindset and developing positive self-talk to help overcome obstacles and create a life of abundance and happiness. Whether you are struggling with self-doubt, fear, or any other limiting beliefs or negative self-talk, this chapter will provide you with the **tools and insights to transform your mindset and achieve your goals.** So, let's dive in and start identifying those mental barriers that are holding you back from your full potential!

Identifying limiting beliefs is the first step towards developing a positive mindset for success in life.

Here are some strategies that can help you identify your limiting beliefs:

Question your thoughts: When you have a negative thought, ask yourself if it is true or if there is evidence to support it. Often, our limiting beliefs are based on assumptions or perceptions that are not necessarily accurate.

Identify patterns: Notice any recurring negative thoughts or beliefs that you have about yourself or your abilities. These patterns can provide insight into your limiting beliefs.
Challenge your beliefs: Once you have identified your limiting beliefs, challenge them. Ask yourself if there is evidence to support them, or if they are simply holding you back from achieving your goals.

Seek feedback: Ask trusted friends or family members for their honest feedback about your beliefs and behaviors. They may be able to provide a different perspective or help you identify areas for growth.

Practice mindfulness: Pay attention to your thoughts and emotions without judgment. Mindfulness can help you identify patterns and beliefs that may be holding you back.

By identifying your limiting beliefs, you can begin to reframe them into positive, empowering thoughts that support your goals and aspirations. With a positive mindset, you can achieve success in all areas of your life. Remember, success is not just about money or material possessions, but also about personal growth, happiness, and fulfillment.

On the other hand, Negative self-talk can have a significant impact on a positive mindset. When we engage in negative self-talk, we reinforce limiting beliefs about ourselves and our abilities, which can lead to feelings of self-doubt, fear, and insecurity. This negative self-talk can also create a self-fulfilling prophecy, where we believe that we are not capable of achieving our goals, and therefore, do not take action toward them.

Negative self-talk can also contribute to negative emotions such as anxiety, stress, and depression, which can further impact our mindset and overall well-being. It can create a cycle of negativity that can be difficult to break, leading to feelings of hopelessness and helplessness.

On the other hand, positive self-talk can help us develop a positive mindset, boost our confidence, and motivate us to take action toward our goals. When we engage in positive self-talk, we reinforce empowering beliefs about ourselves and our abilities, which can lead to feelings of self-assurance and self-efficacy. Positive self-talk can also help us manage negative emotions, increase our resilience, and improve our overall well-being.

Therefore, it is important to be aware of our self-talk and its impact on our mindset. By recognizing negative self-talk and replacing it with positive, empowering thoughts, we can cultivate a positive mindset and achieve success in all areas of our life. Limiting beliefs and negative self-talk can have a significant impact on our thoughts, emotions, and behaviors. Here are some ways they can affect us:

1. **Thoughts:** Limiting beliefs and negative self-talk can impact our thoughts by creating self-doubt and negativity. We may become overly critical of ourselves and others and may struggle with decision-making and problem-solving.

2. **Emotions:** Negative self-talk can lead to negative emotions such as anxiety, stress, and depression. It can create a cycle of negativity that can be difficult to break, leading to feelings of hopelessness and helplessness.

3. **Behaviors:** Limiting beliefs and negative self-talk can impact our behaviors by preventing us from taking action toward our goals. We may avoid challenges and opportunities, and may not take risks for fear of failure.

To overcome limiting beliefs and negative self-talk, here are some practical strategies:

1. **Self-awareness:** Become aware of your self-talk and identify any negative patterns or beliefs. Pay attention to your thoughts and emotions without judgment, and seek to understand the root causes of your limiting beliefs.

2. **Reframe your self-talk:** Once you have identified your limiting beliefs and negative self-talk, reframe them into positive, empowering thoughts. Replace negative self-talk with affirmations and positive statements that support your goals and aspirations.

3. **Practice self-compassion:** Be kind to yourself and practice self-compassion. Remember that everyone makes mistakes and experiences setbacks and that it is okay to fail. Treat yourself with the same kindness and understanding that you would show to a friend.

4. **Seek support:** Surround yourself with positive and supportive people who can help you overcome your limiting beliefs and negative self-talk. Seek a mentor or coach who can provide guidance and accountability.

By identifying and overcoming limiting beliefs and negative self-talk, we can cultivate a positive mindset and achieve success in all areas of our life. It takes time and effort to develop positive self-talk, but with practice, it can become a powerful tool for personal growth and happiness.

Reframing limiting beliefs and negative self-talk

Reframing limiting beliefs and negative self-talk into positive, empowering thoughts can be a powerful tool for personal growth and success. By challenging negative thoughts and replacing them with positive, empowering ones, you can cultivate a positive mindset and achieve your goals.

Strategies like using positive affirmations, practicing gratitude, and visualizing success can help you reframe your thoughts and overcome self-limiting beliefs. With practice and persistence, you can build a strong foundation for personal growth and success. Here are some strategies that can help:

Recognize the limiting belief or negative self-talk: The first step is to recognize and identify the limiting belief or negative self-talk. This requires being mindful and aware of your thoughts and emotions.

Challenge the belief: Once you have identified the limiting belief or negative self-talk, challenge it. Ask yourself if it is based on facts or assumptions. Often, negative self-talk is based on unfounded beliefs or assumptions.

Reframe the belief: Reframe the limiting belief or negative self-talk into a positive, empowering thought. Use positive language and focus on what you can do instead of what you cannot do. For example, instead of "I'm not good enough," reframe it to "I am capable and have the skills to achieve my goals."

Use positive affirmations: Affirmations can help reinforce positive beliefs and attitudes. Use positive affirmations that support your goals and aspirations. Repeat them to yourself regularly.

Practice gratitude: Gratitude can help shift your focus from negative thoughts to positive ones. Take time to reflect on the things you are grateful for and appreciate the positive things in your life.

Visualize success: A visualization is a powerful tool for success. Visualize yourself achieving your goals and living the life you want. This can help reinforce positive beliefs and attitudes.

Reframing limiting beliefs and negative self-talk takes practice and persistence. But with time and effort, you can cultivate a positive mindset and achieve success in all areas of your life. Remember to be patient and kind to yourself, and celebrate your successes along the way.

In the end, Transforming your mindset is essential to achieving your goals and living a fulfilling life. There are several tools and insights that can help you shift your mindset and overcome limiting beliefs. These include identifying and reframing negative self-talk, cultivating self-awareness and self-compassion, setting clear goals, developing positive habits, and seeking support from others. By utilizing these tools and insights, you can create a strong foundation for personal growth and success. Whether you want to improve your career, relationships, or health, transforming your mindset can help you unlock your full potential and achieve your goals.

Chapter 6: Techniques for Overcoming Negative Self-Talk

In chapter 5, we explored the impact of negative self-talk on our mindset and how it can hold us back from achieving our goals. In this chapter, we will delve into practical techniques for overcoming negative self-talk and cultivating a positive, empowering mindset.

Negative self-talk can have a significant impact on a person's mindset, leading to an unhappy life. When a person consistently engages in negative self-talk, they reinforce negative beliefs about themselves and their abilities, which can lead to feelings of inadequacy, low self-esteem, and depression.

Negative self-talk can also create a self-fulfilling prophecy. When a person consistently tells themselves that they cannot do something or that they are not good enough, they may avoid taking action toward their goals, leading to a lack of progress and a sense of stagnation.

Furthermore, negative self-talk can lead to a negative cycle of thoughts, emotions, and behaviors. For example, a person who engages in negative self-talk may feel anxious or depressed, which can lead to negative behaviors such as isolating themselves or engaging in unhealthy habits. These behaviors, in turn, can reinforce negative beliefs and thoughts, perpetuating the cycle of negativity.

Negative self-talk can have a profound impact on a person's mindset and quality of life. To break this cycle, it is essential to recognize and challenge negative self-talk, cultivate self-compassion and self-awareness, and replace negative thoughts with positive, empowering ones. By doing so, a person can develop a positive mindset and achieve greater happiness and fulfillment in life.

Recognizing negative self-talk is the first step in overcoming it. Negative self-talk can be subtle and automatic, and it may take some practice to become aware of it. Here are some examples of negative self-talk:

All-or-nothing thinking: This type of negative self-talk involves seeing things in black and white terms and ignoring shades of gray. For example, "If I don't get an A on this exam, I'm a failure."

Overgeneralization: Overgeneralization involves making sweeping statements based on a single negative event. For example, "I always mess things up" after making a mistake.

Filtering: This involves selectively focusing on the negative aspects of a situation while ignoring the positive aspects. For example, "I got a B on this paper, but I made a few mistakes. It's not good enough."

Personalization: This involves taking personal responsibility for things that are outside of your control. For example, "My boss is always in a bad mood. It must be because of something I did."

Once you can recognize negative self-talk, you can begin to challenge and reframe it. For example, if you catch yourself engaging in all-or-nothing thinking, you can remind yourself that success is not defined by a single event or outcome. You can tell yourself, "I may not have gotten an A on this exam, but I still learned a lot and can work towards improvement."

Similarly, if you find yourself overgeneralizing, you can challenge that thought by reminding yourself that everyone makes mistakes, and one mistake doesn't define your abilities or worth. You can tell yourself, "Making mistakes is a part of the learning process, and I can use this experience to grow and improve."

By recognizing negative self-talk and challenging it with positive, empowering thoughts, you can cultivate a positive mindset and overcome self-limiting beliefs.

The second step is to Challenge a negative self-talk

Challenging negative self-talk involves questioning the accuracy and validity of negative thoughts and beliefs. This is an important step in overcoming negative self-talk and cultivating a more positive and empowering mindset. Here are some examples of how to challenge negative self-talk:

Question the evidence: Ask yourself if the negative thought is based on facts or assumptions. For example, if you find yourself thinking, "I'm not good enough to apply for that job," ask yourself what evidence supports that thought. Is it based on past experiences or assumptions about your abilities?

Look for evidence to the contrary: Once you have identified the evidence that supports the negative thought, look for evidence that contradicts it. For example, if you think, "I always mess things up," look for examples of times when you have succeeded or done well.

Consider alternative explanations: Consider alternative explanations for the situation. For example, if you didn't get the job you applied for, instead of thinking, "I'm not good enough," consider other factors that may have influenced the decision, such as competition or qualifications of other candidates.

Practice cognitive restructuring: Cognitive restructuring involves replacing negative thoughts with positive, empowering ones. For example, if you find yourself thinking, "I'll never be able to do this," reframe the thought as, "This is a challenge, but I can figure it out with effort and determination."

Seek support: Sometimes it can be difficult to challenge negative self-talk on your own. Seek support from friends, family, or a mental health professional who can help you challenge and reframe negative thoughts.

By challenging negative self-talk, you can gain a more balanced and accurate perspective on yourself and the world around you. This can help you overcome self-limiting beliefs and cultivate a more positive and empowering mindset.

Practicing self-compassion is an important technique for overcoming negative self-talk.

Self-compassion involves treating yourself with kindness and understanding, just as you would treat a good friend. Here are some examples of how to practice self-compassion:

Treat yourself as you would treat a friend: Imagine that a friend came to you with the same problem or negative thought that you are experiencing. What would you say to them? How would you comfort and encourage them? Now, try to apply those same words of comfort and encouragement to yourself.

Acknowledge your feelings: It's important to acknowledge and validate your feelings, even if they are uncomfortable or difficult. Instead of criticizing yourself for feeling anxious or down, try to accept your emotions and offer yourself words of kindness and understanding.

Practice mindfulness: Mindfulness involves being present in the moment and observing your thoughts and feelings without judgment. When negative thoughts or feelings arise, try to observe them without getting caught up in them. Recognize that thoughts and emotions come and go, and that they do not define you or your worth.

Reframe negative thoughts: When negative thoughts arise, try to reframe them in a more positive and compassionate light. For example, if you find yourself thinking, "I'm such a failure," reframe the thought as, "I'm going through a difficult time right now, but I'm doing the best I can."

Take care of yourself: Taking care of your physical and emotional needs is an important part of self-compassion. This can include getting enough sleep, eating a balanced diet, exercising regularly, and engaging in activities that bring you joy and fulfillment.

By practicing self-compassion, you can cultivate a more positive and compassionate attitude towards yourself. This can help you overcome negative self-talk and self-limiting beliefs, and lead to greater resilience and well-being.

Surrounding yourself with positivity

Surrounding yourself with positivity is another important technique for overcoming negative self-talk. The people, environments, and media you expose yourself to can have a significant impact on your mindset and emotional well-being. Here are some examples of how to surround yourself with positivity:

Seek out positive relationships: Surround yourself with people who are supportive, positive, and uplifting. This can include friends, family members, mentors, or colleagues who encourage and motivate you.

Create a positive environment: Your physical environment can also impact your mindset. Create a space that feels comfortable, calming, and uplifting. This can include adding plants, uplifting artwork, or comforting lighting.

Limit exposure to negative media: Social media, news outlets, and other forms of media can be a source of negativity and anxiety. Limit your exposure to media that triggers negative self-talk or promotes unrealistic expectations.

Practice gratitude: Focusing on the good things in your life can help shift your mindset towards positivity. Make a daily habit of reflecting on things you are grateful for, no matter how small they may seem.

Engage in positive activities: Engage in activities that bring you joy and fulfillment, whether that's spending time in nature, practicing a hobby, or volunteering for a cause you care about. This can help boost your mood and sense of purpose.

By surrounding yourself with positivity, you can create a more supportive and uplifting environment that can help counteract negative self-talk and self-limiting beliefs. This can help you cultivate a more positive and resilient mindset, and lead to greater success and well-being.

In conclusion, Chapter 6 explores various techniques for overcoming negative self-talk, which can have a profound impact on our thoughts, emotions, and behaviors. By recognizing negative self-talk, challenging it, practicing self-compassion, and surrounding ourselves with positivity, we can transform our mindset and achieve our goals.

Recognizing negative self-talk is the first step in overcoming it. This involves becoming aware of the negative messages we tell ourselves and how they impact our well-being. Challenging negative self-talk involves questioning the accuracy and validity of these messages and reframing them in a more positive and empowering light.

Practicing self-compassion involves treating ourselves with kindness and understanding, just as we would treat a good friend. This can help us accept our emotions and experiences, and cultivate a more positive and compassionate attitude toward ourselves.

Surrounding ourselves with positivity can also help counteract negative self-talk and self-limiting beliefs. This includes seeking out positive relationships, creating a positive environment, limiting exposure to negative media, practicing gratitude, and engaging in positive activities.

By applying these techniques, we can transform our mindset and achieve greater success and well-being. We can learn to overcome self-doubt and self-sabotage and cultivate a more positive and resilient attitude toward ourselves and our goals.

Chapter 7: Changing Your Beliefs to Change Your Life

In the previous chapters, we discussed the power of mindset and how it can impact your success in life. One critical aspect of your mindset is your beliefs. Your beliefs shape your perception of the world and guide your actions and decisions. They are the foundation of your mindset and can either propel you toward success or hold you back.

In this chapter, we'll explore how changing your beliefs can change your life. We'll look at how limiting beliefs can hinder your success and how to identify and overcome them. We'll also discuss how to cultivate positive beliefs that can help you achieve your goals.

The Power of Beliefs

Your beliefs shape your reality. They are the lenses through which you view the world and determine what you see, how you interpret events, and how you react to them. Your beliefs also influence your thoughts, emotions, and behaviors. For example, if you believe that you're not good enough, you may feel insecure and act in ways that reinforce that belief, such as avoiding challenges or procrastinating.

Your beliefs can be empowering or limiting. Empowering beliefs help you to see opportunities and possibilities, take risks, and persevere in the face of challenges. Limiting beliefs, on the other hand, hold you back by creating fear, self-doubt, and negative self-talk. They can lead to a fixed mindset that makes you resistant to change and growth.

Identifying Limiting Beliefs

To change your beliefs, you first need to identify the ones that are holding you back. Here are some common limiting beliefs:

1. I'm not smart enough/ talented enough/ good enough.
2. I'll never be able to do that.
3. Success is only for lucky people.
4. I'm too old/young/fat/thin/short/tall to do that.
5. It's too late for me to start over.
6. I'll never be able to make enough money.
7. I'm not the kind of person who can be successful.

These beliefs are often deeply ingrained and can be challenging to overcome. However, by acknowledging them, you can start to challenge their validity and replace them with more empowering beliefs.

Overcoming Limiting Beliefs

To overcome limiting beliefs, you need to challenge their validity and replace them with more empowering beliefs. Here are some steps to help you do that:

1. Identify the belief: Start by identifying the limiting belief that is holding you back. Write it down and be specific.
2. Challenge the belief: Ask yourself if the belief is true. Is there evidence that supports it? Is it based on facts or just assumptions? Is it a belief that you've inherited from others?
3. Replace the belief: Once you've challenged the belief, replace it with a more empowering one. For example, if you believe that you're not good enough, replace it with "I am capable of achieving my goals."
4. Repeat the new belief: Repeat your new belief to yourself regularly. Write it down and put it in a place where you can see it daily. Visualize yourself living with this new belief.

5. Take action: Finally, take action based on your new belief. Challenge yourself to step outside your comfort zone and take risks. Celebrate your successes, no matter how small.

Cultivating Positive Beliefs

In addition to overcoming limiting beliefs, it's essential to cultivate positive beliefs that will help you achieve your goals. Here are some examples of positive beliefs:

1. I am capable of achieving my goals.
2. Failure is an opportunity to learn and grow.
3. Success is within my reach if I work hard and persevere.
4. I am in control of my life and my destiny.
5. There are plenty of opportunities for

Changing Your Beliefs

Changing your beliefs means consciously and intentionally altering the ideas, assumptions, and attitudes that you hold about yourself, others, and the world around you. Beliefs are often deeply ingrained and may have been formed over many years of experiences, feedback, and conditioning.

Changing your beliefs requires a willingness to challenge limiting beliefs, reframe negative self-talk, and replace them with empowering beliefs that align with your goals and values. This process often involves introspection, self-awareness, and a commitment to personal growth and development. Techniques for changing beliefs may include affirmations, visualization, cognitive restructuring, mindfulness, and working with a therapist or coach.

Changing your beliefs can have a profound impact on your life. It can boost your confidence, increase your motivation, and help you overcome obstacles that were once perceived as insurmountable. By changing your beliefs, you can create a more positive mindset and become more resilient, adaptable, and open to new opportunities. Ultimately, changing your beliefs can help you achieve your goals, find greater fulfillment and meaning, and lead a more successful and happy life.

Maintaining Your New Beliefs

Maintaining your new beliefs means continuing to adopt and apply your new positive beliefs over time, even when faced with challenges, setbacks, or negative thoughts. It involves building a lasting commitment to your new perspective and actively seeking ways to reinforce and strengthen your new beliefs.

Here are some strategies for maintaining your new beliefs:

Practice Self-Awareness: Be aware of your thoughts, emotions, and behaviors. When you notice negative self-talk or doubts creeping in, take a moment to pause, reflect, and challenge those thoughts. Use positive affirmations and visualization to reinforce your new beliefs.

Seek Out Positive Environments: Surround yourself with people and environments that support your new beliefs. Seek out relationships and activities that align with your values and reinforce your positive mindset.

Celebrate Your Progress: Recognize and celebrate your accomplishments, no matter how small they may seem. Celebrating your progress can help reinforce your new beliefs and motivate you to continue on your path.

Embrace Failure as a Learning Opportunity: View failure as an opportunity to learn and grow, rather than a setback. Use each failure as a chance to adjust your approach and refine your beliefs, and apply those lessons learned to future endeavors.

Stay Committed to Personal Growth: Maintain a commitment to personal growth and development. Continuously seek out new opportunities to learn, challenge yourself, and expand your beliefs. This can include reading books, attending seminars, or working with a coach or therapist.

The main goal of changing your beliefs is to cultivate a growth mindset. A growth mindset is a belief that you can develop and improve your abilities through hard work, dedication, and perseverance. It's the opposite of a fixed mindset, which is the belief that your abilities and intelligence are set and cannot be changed.

When you have a growth mindset, you're more likely to take on challenges, learn from failure, and keep going even when things get tough. You see setbacks as opportunities to learn and grow, and you believe that your effort and determination can lead to success.

Changing your beliefs to lead a growth mindset involves identifying and challenging limiting beliefs and replacing them with positive and empowering ones. It requires a willingness to step outside your comfort zone and take risks, even when you're afraid of failing.

To cultivate a growth mindset, you need to embrace the idea that your abilities and intelligence are not fixed but can be developed through effort and practice. You need to believe in your potential and focus on growth and learning rather than on proving yourself or seeking validation from others.

One way to develop a growth mindset is to adopt a "yet" mentality. Instead of saying "I can't do that," say "I can't do that yet, but I'm willing to learn and practice." This subtle shift in language can make a big difference in how you approach challenges and setbacks.

Overall, changing your beliefs to lead a growth mindset requires a commitment to growth and learning. It involves challenging limiting beliefs, embracing the power of effort and practice, and focusing on the process rather than the outcome. With a growth mindset, you can achieve your goals, overcome obstacles, and lead a fulfilling and successful life.

Moreover, Changing your beliefs can have a significant impact on your life, leading to greater success, happiness, and fulfillment. Here are a few ways that changing your beliefs can help you achieve these goals:

Greater Confidence: When you change limiting beliefs to empowering ones, you start to believe in yourself more. You see yourself as capable and deserving of success, which can boost your confidence and self-esteem. With greater confidence, you're more likely to take on challenges, pursue your goals, and overcome obstacles.

More Positive Mindset: Changing your beliefs can help you cultivate a more positive mindset. By focusing on the good things in life and letting go of negative thoughts and emotions, you can reduce stress and anxiety and increase your overall sense of well-being. A positive mindset can also help you see opportunities instead of obstacles, leading to greater success in your personal and professional life.

Improved Relationships: Changing your beliefs can also improve your relationships with others. By letting go of limiting beliefs about yourself and others, you can become more accepting, compassionate, and empathetic. This can lead to deeper connections, more fulfilling relationships, and a greater sense of belonging and community.

Increased Resilience: Changing your beliefs can also make you more resilient in the face of challenges and setbacks. By adopting a growth mindset and focusing on learning and growth, you can bounce back from failures and setbacks more quickly and effectively. This resilience can help you overcome obstacles and achieve your goals, even in the face of adversity.

Changing your beliefs can lead to a more successful and happy life by boosting your confidence, cultivating a positive mindset, improving your relationships, and increasing your resilience. It requires a willingness to challenge limiting beliefs, embrace growth and learning, and focus on the good things in life. With time and effort, you can change your beliefs and create the life you desire.

How to Banishing an old belief

Banishing an old belief involves a deliberate and conscious effort to identify and challenge the limiting belief and replace it with a more empowering belief. Here are some steps you can take to banish an old belief:

Identify the Belief: The first step is to identify the old belief that is holding you back. Recognize the negative self-talk or thought patterns that are reinforcing the belief.

Challenge the Belief: Once you have identified the belief, challenge it. Ask yourself if it is really true, and consider alternative perspectives or evidence that contradicts the belief. This can help you break down the belief and see it for what it really is - a limiting belief that is not grounded in reality.

Reframe the Belief: Once you have challenged the old belief, reframe it into a more empowering belief. Focus on creating a positive, affirming statement that aligns with your values and goals. For example, if your old belief was "I am not smart enough," you could reframe it as "I am capable of learning and growing, and I can achieve my goals through hard work and dedication."

Repeat the New Belief: Repeat the new belief to yourself frequently, preferably in the present tense, and with emotion and conviction. This will help reinforce the new belief and create new neural pathways in your brain that support the positive belief.

Take Action: Finally, take action toward your new belief.

In conclusion, Changing your beliefs is a powerful way to transform your life. By recognizing and challenging limiting beliefs, reframing negative thoughts, seeking out new experiences, and cultivating self-awareness, you can begin to change your mindset and unlock your full potential. The process of changing your beliefs requires effort and perseverance, but the rewards can be significant in terms of personal growth, achievement, and fulfillment.

Chapter 8: The Power of Visualization and Affirmations

Visualization and affirmations are powerful tools that can help individuals achieve their goals and cultivate a positive mindset. By combining these techniques, individuals can create a mental image of their desired outcome and reinforce positive beliefs about their abilities.

Visualization is the process of creating a mental image or scenario of a desired outcome. By visualizing success, individuals can focus their minds on what they want to achieve and increase their motivation to take action toward their goals. Visualization can be done in a variety of ways, including guided meditations, mental rehearsals, and visualization boards.

Mental rehearsal involves visualizing oneself successfully completing a specific task or achieving a goal. For example, a musician may mentally rehearse a performance by visualizing themselves playing flawlessly, hearing the audience's applause, and feeling the satisfaction of a successful performance. This technique can help individuals build confidence and reduce anxiety, which can ultimately lead to better performance.

Visualization boards, also known as vision boards or dream boards, are physical representations of a person's goals and desires. They can be created using images, words, and symbols that represent what the person wants to achieve. By placing the visualization board in a prominent location, individuals are reminded of their goals and motivated to take action toward achieving them.

Affirmations are positive statements that individuals repeat to themselves to reinforce positive beliefs about themselves and their abilities. By using affirmations, individuals can shift their mindset from a negative or self-limiting perspective to a positive and empowering one.

Affirmations can be used in a variety of ways, such as repeating them out loud, writing them down, or incorporating them into a daily meditation practice. The key is to choose affirmations that resonate with the individual and reflect the positive change they want to see in themselves.

For example, an individual who struggles with self-confidence may use affirmations such as "I am capable and confident in all that I do" or "I trust in my abilities and know that I can succeed." By repeating these affirmations, the individual can reinforce positive beliefs about themselves and overcome self-doubt.

Visualization and affirmations can be powerful tools for cultivating a positive mindset and achieving success. By incorporating these techniques into their daily routine, individuals can focus their minds on their goals, increase their motivation to take action and reinforce positive beliefs about themselves and their abilities.

The power of visualization and affirmations can help individuals develop a positive and productive mindset for success in several ways:

1. **Clarifying Goals:** Visualization can help individuals clarify their goals by creating a vivid mental image of what they want to achieve. This can help them focus on their priorities and develop a clear plan of action. Affirmations can reinforce positive beliefs about their ability to achieve these goals.

2. **Boosting Motivation:** Visualization can increase motivation by creating a sense of excitement and anticipation about the future. By visualizing success, individuals can feel more confident in their ability to achieve their goals, and this can increase their motivation to take action.

3. **Building Confidence:** Visualization can help individuals build confidence by mentally rehearsing successful outcomes. Affirmations can also help individuals overcome negative self-talk and replace it with positive self-talk, which can build confidence and self-esteem.

4. **Overcoming Obstacles:** Visualization can help individuals overcome obstacles by creating a mental image of themselves successfully navigating challenging situations. Affirmations can also help individuals stay focused on their goals and believe in their ability to overcome setbacks and obstacles.

5. **Enhancing Focus:** Visualization and affirmations can help individuals stay focused on their goals and maintain a positive mindset even in the face of adversity. By regularly visualizing success and repeating positive affirmations, individuals can strengthen their mindset and stay motivated to achieve their goals.

The power of visualization and affirmations can help individuals develop a positive and productive mindset for success by clarifying goals, boosting motivation, building confidence, overcoming obstacles, and enhancing focus. By incorporating these techniques into their daily routine, individuals can cultivate a strong mindset that supports their success in all areas of life.

One inspirational story that illustrates the power of visualization and affirmations is the story of Jim Carrey, a successful actor and comedian. As a struggling young comedian in the 1980s, Carrey faced numerous setbacks and rejections. However, he believed in the power of visualization and affirmations, and he used these techniques to help him achieve his goals.

Carrey wrote himself a check for $10 million, dated it five years in the future, and kept it in his wallet as a constant reminder of his goal to become a successful actor. He also spent time visualizing himself as a successful actor, imagining himself receiving awards and critical acclaim.

Despite facing numerous setbacks and rejections, Carrey refused to give up on his dreams. He continued to work hard and believe in himself, using visualization and affirmations to stay focused and motivated. And eventually, his hard work paid off. In 1994, he starred in the hit movie "Ace Ventura: Pet Detective," which launched his career as a successful actor and comedian.

Looking back on his success, Carrey has credited the power of visualization and affirmations for helping him achieve his goals. He once said, "You can't just visualize and go eat a sandwich. You have to work hard. But visualizing is a powerful tool that can help you achieve your goals."

Carrey's story is a powerful reminder of the importance of belief in oneself and the power of visualization and affirmations. By staying focused on his goals and believing in himself, Carrey was able to overcome obstacles and achieve success beyond his wildest dreams.

Here's how you can create visualization and affirmation habits for yourself to get a highly successful mindset.

Creating a powerful visualization and affirmation practice requires intention, commitment, and consistency. Here are some steps you can follow to create a practice that works for you:

1. **Set clear goals:** The first step in creating a powerful visualization and affirmation practice is to set clear goals. Make sure your goals are specific, measurable, and achievable. Write them down and review them regularly.

2. **Visualize success:** Once you have set your goals, spend time visualizing yourself achieving them. Use all your senses to create a vivid mental image of yourself succeeding. Imagine how you will feel, what you will see, hear, and smell, and how you will celebrate your success.

3. **Use positive affirmations:** Affirmations are positive statements that help you reinforce positive beliefs about yourself and your ability to achieve your goals. Write down positive affirmations that resonate with you, and repeat them to yourself regularly. You can also record them and listen to them throughout the day.

4. **Make it a habit:** To create lasting change, make visualization and affirmations a daily habit. Set aside a specific time each day to practice, and be consistent. The more you practice, the more powerful your practice will become.

5. **Believe in yourself:** Finally, believe in yourself and your ability to achieve your goals. Trust the process and have faith that your efforts will pay off. Remember that visualization and affirmations are tools to help you create a positive and productive mindset, but ultimately, success comes from taking action and working hard.

Creating a powerful visualization and affirmation practice takes time and effort, but the benefits are well worth it. By using these tools to cultivate a positive and productive mindset, you can achieve success in all areas of your life.

In conclusion, the power of visualization and affirmations can be a game-changer when it comes to developing a positive and productive mindset for success. By using these powerful tools, individuals can clarify their goals, boost motivation, build confidence, overcome obstacles, and enhance focus.

Creating a powerful visualization and affirmation practice takes intention, commitment, and consistency, but the benefits are well worth the effort. With practice, individuals can cultivate a strong mindset that supports their success in all areas of life.

Remember that visualization and affirmations are not a substitute for action and hard work, but rather a tool to help you stay focused and motivated on your goals. By combining visualization and affirmations with consistent action, individuals can create a powerful formula for success.

So, start using visualization and affirmations in your daily routine, and watch as your mindset shifts towards a more positive and productive outlook, propelling you toward success in all areas of your life. The power to achieve your goals is within you; all you need to do is believe it and visualize it.

Part 3: Goal-Setting and Success Strategies

Chapter 9: Setting and Achieving Goals

Setting and achieving goals is a crucial aspect of developing a positive and productive mindset for success. Without clear goals, it can be challenging to stay focused and motivated, and individuals may find themselves drifting aimlessly through life.

In this chapter, we will explore the importance of setting and achieving goals, the benefits of doing so, and the steps individuals can take to set and achieve their goals.

The Importance of Setting Goals

Setting goals is important for several reasons. Firstly, it provides direction and purpose in life. When individuals have a clear idea of what they want to achieve, they are more likely to focus their attention and energy on activities that will help them reach their goals. This sense of direction can help individuals stay motivated and avoid drifting aimlessly through life.

Secondly, setting goals provides a roadmap for success. By breaking down a larger goal into smaller, more manageable tasks, individuals can create a step-by-step plan for achieving their desired outcome. This can help to make a daunting goal feel more achievable and increase the likelihood of success.

Thirdly, setting and achieving goals can boost self-confidence and self-esteem. When individuals accomplish what they set out to do, they feel a sense of pride and accomplishment, which can help to improve their self-image and overall outlook on life.

Lastly, setting goals can help individuals prioritize their time and resources. When individuals have a clear idea of what they want to achieve, they can better allocate their time, money, and energy toward activities that will help them reach their goals. This can increase productivity and efficiency and help individuals achieve their desired outcomes more quickly.

Setting goals is essential for providing direction and purpose, creating a roadmap for success, boosting self-confidence and self-esteem, and prioritizing time and resources toward activities that will help individuals achieve their desired outcomes.

The Benefits of Setting Goals

Setting and achieving goals offers many benefits that can help individuals improve their personal and professional lives. Here are some of the key benefits of setting goals:

1. **Increased Motivation:** When individuals set goals, they have a clear purpose and direction, which can increase motivation and drive. Having a specific target to aim for can give individuals a sense of purpose and inspire them to take action towards achieving their goals.
2. **Improved Focus:** Goals help individuals to focus their attention and energy on what is essential. By setting clear objectives, individuals can avoid distractions and prioritize activities that are aligned with their goals. This can increase focus and productivity, leading to better outcomes.
3. **Greater Self-Confidence:** Achieving goals can boost self-confidence and self-esteem. When individuals accomplish what they set out to do, they feel a sense of pride and accomplishment, which can improve their self-image and overall outlook on life.

4. **Increased Productivity:** Goals provide a clear roadmap for success. By breaking down a larger goal into smaller, more manageable tasks, individuals can create a step-by-step plan for achieving their desired outcome. This can increase productivity and efficiency, as individuals can focus on completing one task at a time.

5. **Greater Sense of Control:** Setting goals can help individuals feel more in control of their lives. By identifying what they want to achieve and creating a plan for how to get there, individuals can take ownership of their goals and feel empowered to take action towards achieving them.

6. **Improved Decision-Making:** When individuals have clear goals, they can use them as a guide for making decisions. By considering how their actions align with their goals, individuals can make more informed decisions that are aligned with their long-term objectives.

Setting and achieving goals offers many benefits, including increased motivation, improved focus, greater self-confidence, increased productivity, a greater sense of control, and improved decision-making. By setting clear objectives and creating a plan for achieving them, individuals can take control of their lives and achieve their desired outcomes.

Steps to Setting and Achieving Goals

Setting and achieving goals involves a series of steps that individuals can follow to increase their chances of success. Discover the importance of setting goals and learn how to achieve them with our expert guide. From defining your objectives to developing a plan, taking action, and celebrating success, our step-by-step approach will help you stay motivated, focused, and in control of your life. Start setting and achieving your goals today and unlock your true potential. Here are the key steps to setting and achieving goals:

1. **Define Your Goal:** The first step in setting a goal is to define it clearly. This means identifying what you want to achieve, why it is important to you, and what specific outcome you are aiming for.

2. **Set SMART Goals:** SMART is an acronym that stands for Specific, Measurable, Achievable, Relevant, and Time-bound. Setting SMART goals means creating goals that are specific, measurable, achievable, relevant to your life, and time-bound.

3. **Develop a Plan:** Once you have set your goal, develop a plan for achieving it. This means breaking your goal down into smaller, more manageable tasks, and identifying the steps you need to take to reach your desired outcome.

4. **Take Action:** Once you have a plan, take action toward achieving your goal. This means committing to the steps you have identified and following through on your plan.

5. **Monitor Progress:** Regularly monitor your progress toward your goal. This means tracking your progress, assessing how well you are doing, and adjusting your plan as needed.

6. **Stay Motivated:** Staying motivated is essential for achieving your goals. This means focusing on the benefits of achieving your goal, celebrating your progress, and staying positive in the face of challenges.

7. **Celebrate Success:** When you achieve your goal, take the time to celebrate your success. This means acknowledging

your accomplishment, recognizing your hard work, and taking pride in your achievement.

Setting and achieving goals involves defining your goal, setting SMART goals, developing a plan, taking action, monitoring progress, staying motivated, and celebrating success. By following these steps, individuals can increase their chances of success and achieve their desired outcomes.

One of the most famous examples of goal-setting leading to success is the story of Roger Bannister, the first man to run a mile in under four minutes. In 1952, experts believed that it was physically impossible for a human being to run a mile in under four minutes. However, Bannister refused to believe this, and he set himself the goal of achieving this seemingly impossible feat.

Bannister trained tirelessly, pushing himself to the limit every day. He visualized himself running the mile in under four minutes, and he wrote this goal down on a piece of paper that he kept in his pocket at all times. On May 6, 1954, Bannister finally achieved his goal, running the mile in three minutes and 59.4 seconds.

Bannister's achievement inspired countless others to set ambitious goals for themselves, and within a year, more than a dozen runners had broken the four-minute barrier. Bannister's example showed that setting a clear goal, working hard, and believing in oneself can lead to incredible achievements, even in the face of seemingly insurmountable obstacles.

Conclusion

Setting and achieving goals is a crucial aspect of developing a positive and productive mindset for success. By setting clear, measurable goals and creating a plan for achieving them, individuals can stay focused, motivated, and on track toward achieving their desired outcomes.

Remember that achieving your goals takes hard work, commitment, and dedication, but the rewards are well worth the effort. With a positive mindset and a clear roadmap for success, individuals can achieve their goals and realize their full potential in all areas of life.

Chapter 10: The Importance of Persistence and Resilience

In life, we will all face obstacles and setbacks. Whether it's a failed business venture, a relationship gone sour, or a personal tragedy, adversity is a part of the human experience. However, it is not the obstacles themselves that determine our success or failure, but rather our response to them. In this chapter, we will explore the importance of persistence and resilience in overcoming obstacles and achieving our goals.

Section 1: The Power of Persistence

Persistence can be defined as the act of continuing to pursue a goal or objective despite facing obstacles, setbacks, or failures. It is a vital quality that is required for achieving success, as it helps individuals to maintain their focus, motivation, and determination when faced with challenges.

The importance of persistence in achieving success cannot be overstated. Those who are persistent are more likely to overcome setbacks and failures, and are better equipped to navigate the ups and downs of life. Persistence helps individuals to stay focused on their goals, even when faced with distractions or competing priorities. It also helps individuals to develop a growth mindset, where they see setbacks and failures as opportunities for learning and growth rather than as signs of weakness or defeat.

Ultimately, persistence is a key ingredient in achieving success, as it helps individuals to stay committed to their goals and to keep moving forward even when faced with challenges or obstacles. Without persistence, many of the world's greatest achievements would never have been realized, and individuals would be much less likely to achieve their full potential.

There are countless examples of successful individuals who persisted through failure and setbacks on their path to achieving success. Here are just a few examples:

1. **Thomas Edison:** Edison is widely regarded as one of the most successful inventors in history, having invented the phonograph, the motion picture camera, and, of course, the light bulb. However, Edison faced many setbacks and failures throughout his career, including over 1,000 unsuccessful attempts to create a working light bulb. Despite these setbacks, he remained persistent and eventually succeeded in creating a working light bulb, forever changing the world.

2. **J.K. Rowling:** Rowling is the author of the wildly successful Harry Potter series, but before her success, she faced numerous rejections from publishers who didn't believe in her work. Despite these setbacks, she persisted in pursuing her dream and eventually found a publisher who was willing to take a chance on her. Today, her books have sold over 500 million copies worldwide.

3. **Michael Jordan:** Jordan is widely regarded as one of the greatest basketball players of all time, but he faced numerous setbacks throughout his career. He was cut from his high school basketball team and faced numerous defeats and setbacks on his way to becoming a professional player. However, he remained persistent, practicing tirelessly and pushing himself to become the best player he could be. Today, he is a six-time NBA champion and a global icon.

4. **Oprah Winfrey:** Winfrey is one of the most successful talk show hosts and media moguls of all time, but she faced

numerous obstacles on her path to success. She grew up in poverty and faced abuse and neglect as a child. However, she remained persistent, working hard to build a career in media and eventually becoming one of the most influential figures in the industry.

These examples demonstrate that persistence is a key ingredient in achieving success and that even the most successful individuals face setbacks and failures on their path to achieving their goals. It is the ability to persist through these challenges that sets them apart and ultimately leads to their success.

Developing and maintaining persistence is essential for achieving success in any area of life. Here are some strategies for developing and maintaining persistence in the face of obstacles:

1. **Set clear goals:** Having a clear and specific goal in mind can help you stay focused and motivated when faced with obstacles. Break down your larger goal into smaller, achievable milestones and celebrate each accomplishment along the way.
2. **Develop a growth mindset:** Embrace challenges and view failures as opportunities for growth and learning. Believe in your ability to improve and persist despite setbacks.
3. **Seek support:** Surround yourself with positive, supportive people who believe in your abilities and can offer encouragement and guidance when needed.
4. Practice self-care: Take care of your physical and mental health by getting enough sleep, eating a healthy diet, and engaging in activities that help you relax and recharge.
5. **Stay flexible:** Be willing to adapt and adjust your approach when faced with obstacles. Sometimes a different approach or strategy may be needed to overcome a challenge.

6. **Stay organized and track progress:** Keep track of your progress and make adjustments as necessary. This can help you stay motivated and focused on your goals.
7. **Celebrate successes:** Celebrate your successes, no matter how small. Recognize and acknowledge your accomplishments to help you stay motivated and persistent.

Remember that persistence is a skill that can be developed and improved over time. With the right mindset and strategies, you can overcome obstacles and achieve your goals.

Section 2: The Importance of Resilience

Resilience refers to the ability to recover from and adapt to adversity, challenges, and setbacks. It is the capacity to bounce back from difficult experiences and remain focused on one's goals, despite obstacles or setbacks. Resilience is important because it allows individuals to overcome adversity and build strength and confidence in their ability to cope with challenges.

In life, everyone faces challenges and setbacks, whether they are personal or professional. Resilience allows individuals to maintain their sense of well-being and continue to pursue their goals, even when faced with difficult situations. By developing resilience, individuals can learn to respond to challenges in a healthy and adaptive way, rather than becoming overwhelmed or discouraged.

Resilience is not just about bouncing back from difficult experiences, but also about learning and growing from them. When faced with adversity, resilient individuals are able to draw on their inner strength and resources to find new ways to cope and adapt to the situation. Through this process, they can develop new skills, insights, and perspectives that can help them navigate future challenges more effectively.

Resilience is a critical skill that allows individuals to bounce back from adversity, cope with stress, and thrive in the face of challenges. Here are some key reasons why resilience is important:

1. **Overcoming obstacles:** Resilience allows individuals to overcome obstacles and setbacks, and to keep moving forward towards their goals. It helps individuals to stay focused and motivated, even when faced with adversity.

2. **Coping with stress:** Resilience is essential for coping with stress and maintaining well-being. It allows individuals to manage the demands of daily life without becoming overwhelmed or burned out.

3. **Adapting to change:** Resilience enables individuals to adapt to changes and transitions, such as moving to a new city, changing jobs, or experiencing a loss. It allows individuals to stay flexible and open to new opportunities, even in the face of uncertainty.

4. **Building confidence and self-esteem:** Resilience is linked to greater confidence and self-esteem. By overcoming challenges and setbacks, individuals can develop a sense of mastery and self-efficacy, which can help them to tackle future challenges with greater confidence.

5. **Enhancing relationships:** Resilience is also important for building strong and healthy relationships. Individuals who are resilient are better able to communicate effectively, resolve conflicts, and build trust with others.

Overall, resilience is an essential quality for achieving success and maintaining well-being in the face of adversity. By developing resilience, individuals can build the skills and confidence needed to overcome obstacles and thrive in both their personal and professional lives.

Section 3: Overcoming Obstacles with Persistence and Resilience

Overcoming obstacles is a critical part of achieving success in life. However, obstacles and setbacks are an inevitable part of any journey, and it is important to develop persistence and resilience to overcome them. In this section, we will explore how persistence and resilience can help individuals overcome obstacles and achieve their goals.

1. **Persistence in the face of obstacles**

Persistence is the ability to keep moving forward towards a goal, even when faced with obstacles and setbacks. It is an essential quality for achieving success, as obstacles and setbacks are inevitable on any journey. Here are some strategies for developing persistence:

- **Set specific goals:** Having clear and specific goals can help individuals stay focused and motivated, even in the face of obstacles.

- **Break goals down into manageable steps:** Breaking down larger goals into smaller, more manageable steps can help individuals stay motivated and make progress even when faced with obstacles.

- **Stay committed:** Committing to a goal and refusing to give up, even when faced with setbacks, is a key aspect of persistence.

- **Stay positive:** Maintaining a positive attitude and focusing on progress, rather than setbacks, can help individuals maintain motivation and keep moving forward.

2. Resilience in the face of adversity

Resilience is the ability to bounce back from adversity, cope with stress, and thrive in the face of challenges. It is an essential skill for overcoming obstacles and achieving success. Here are some strategies for developing resilience:

- **Practice self-care:** Taking care of oneself, through activities such as exercise, meditation, and spending time with loved ones, can help build resilience and cope with stress.

- **Develop a growth mindset:** Adopting a growth mindset, in which setbacks and failures are viewed as opportunities for learning and growth, can help build resilience and overcome obstacles.

- **Build a support system:** Having a strong support system, whether it is friends, family, or a professional network, can help individuals cope with stress and bounce back from adversity.

- **Embrace change:** Embracing change and being flexible in the face of challenges can help individuals adapt and overcome obstacles.

Overall, Persistence and resilience are crucial skills for achieving success and overcoming adversity. Persistence allows individuals to keep moving forward towards their goals, even when faced with obstacles and setbacks. Resilience enables individuals to bounce back from adversity, cope with stress, and thrive in the face of challenges. Both skills are necessary for achieving success in any area of life, as obstacles and setbacks are inevitable on any journey. By developing persistence and resilience, individuals can stay motivated, focused, and adaptable in the face of adversity, ultimately achieving their goals and thriving in life.

In life, we are often faced with obstacles and setbacks that can make it difficult to achieve our goals. However, by cultivating persistence and resilience, we can overcome these challenges and pursue our goals with determination and perseverance.

Persistence is the ability to keep moving forward towards a goal, even when faced with obstacles and setbacks. It is the key to achieving success in any area of life, as it allows us to stay focused and motivated despite the challenges we may encounter along the way.

Resilience is the ability to bounce back from adversity, cope with stress, and thrive in the face of challenges. It is a crucial skill for overcoming obstacles and achieving success, as it enables us to adapt to changing circumstances and continue to pursue our goals, even in the face of adversity.
By developing persistence and resilience, you can overcome obstacles and achieve your goals, no matter how difficult they may seem. You can stay motivated, focused, and adaptable, and ultimately thrive in life.

So, I encourage you to cultivate persistence and resilience in your own life. Set clear and specific goals, break them down into manageable steps, and stay committed to achieving them. Practice self-care, adopt a growth mindset, build a strong support system, and embrace change. With persistence and resilience, you can overcome any obstacle and achieve success in any area of life.

Remember, the journey towards success may not always be easy, but with determination and perseverance, you can overcome any challenge and achieve your dreams. So, go out there and pursue your goals with persistence and resilience. You have the power to make your dreams a reality.

Chapter 11: The Benefits of Taking Action and Embracing Failure

In this chapter, we will explore the benefits of taking action and embracing failure. Many people are held back by fear of failure, which can prevent them from taking action toward their goals. However, taking action and embracing failure can lead to personal and professional growth, increased resilience, and ultimately, greater success in life.

Section 1: The Benefits of Taking Action

Taking action provides opportunities to develop new skills or improve existing ones. When we take action, we learn through experience and practice, which helps us acquire new skills and knowledge that we can use in various aspects of our lives.

When we take action toward our goals and achieve small successes along the way, it builds our confidence and self-esteem. This allows us to believe in our abilities and encourages us to take more risks and challenges.

Taking action often involves stepping outside our comfort zone and trying new things. This helps us expand our comfort zone and become more resilient and adaptable to changes and challenges in our personal and professional lives.

Taking action opens up new opportunities and experiences that we may not have encountered otherwise. It allows us to explore different paths and discover new passions, which can lead to personal and professional growth.

Taking action creates momentum toward our goals and increases our motivation to continue taking action. This helps us stay focused and committed to our goals, even when faced with obstacles or setbacks.

Taking action is crucial for achieving success and personal growth. Here are some benefits of taking action:

1. **Creates Momentum:** When we take action, it creates momentum toward our goals. Each step we take toward our goal increases our motivation and makes it easier to continue taking action.
2. **Builds Confidence:** Taking action and achieving small successes along the way can build our confidence and self-esteem. It helps us believe in our abilities and encourages us to take more risks.
3. **Generates New Opportunities:** Taking action opens up new opportunities and experiences that we may not have encountered otherwise. It allows us to explore different paths and discover new passions.
4. **Improves Decision-Making:** When we take action, we are forced to make decisions and take responsibility for our choices. This helps us improve our decision-making skills and become more decisive in our lives.
5. **Overcomes Procrastination:** Procrastination can be a major obstacle to success. By taking action, we can overcome procrastination and prevent it from holding us back.
6. **Enhances Learning:** Taking action allows us to learn from our experiences, both positive and negative. It helps us develop new skills and gain knowledge that we can apply in other areas of our lives.

Overall, taking action is essential for personal and professional growth. It allows us to overcome our fears, achieve our goals, and become the best version of ourselves.

Section 2: The Benefits of Embracing Failure

Failure can be defined as the lack of success or the inability to achieve a desired outcome. It can be a frustrating and demotivating experience, but it can also be an opportunity for growth and learning.

When we reframe failure as an opportunity for growth, we shift our mindset to view failure as a natural part of the learning process. Instead of seeing failure as a reflection of our abilities or worth, we see it as a chance to reflect on our actions, learn from our mistakes, and make improvements for the future.

Reframing failure as an opportunity for growth can help us:

1. **Learn from Mistakes:** When we view failure as an opportunity for growth, we can reflect on what went wrong and identify areas for improvement. This helps us learn from our mistakes and avoid making the same ones in the future.

2. **Build Resilience:** Reframing failure as an opportunity for growth helps us develop resilience and perseverance. We learn to embrace challenges and setbacks as opportunities for growth, rather than as roadblocks to our success.

3. **Foster Creativity:** Failure often requires us to think outside the box and come up with new solutions to problems. This helps us develop our creativity and innovation skills, which can benefit us in all areas of life.

4. **Develop Grit:** Grit refers to the ability to persevere and maintain focus on long-term goals, even in the face of challenges and setbacks. Reframing failure as an opportunity for growth helps us develop grit and stay

committed to our goals, despite obstacles.

Overall, reframing failure as an opportunity for growth allows us to approach challenges with a positive and growth-oriented mindset. It helps us learn from our mistakes, develop resilience, and ultimately achieve greater success in our personal and professional lives.

The importance of embracing failure as a necessary step towards success lies in the fact that failure is inevitable in the pursuit of success. No one can achieve success without experiencing failure along the way. Failure can be viewed as an opportunity for growth and learning, rather than something to be ashamed of or feared. By embracing failure, individuals can shift their mindset and focus on the lessons learned, rather than dwelling on the negative emotions that come with it.

Embracing failure also means taking risks and stepping out of one's comfort zone, which can lead to personal and professional growth. It allows individuals to discover new approaches and methods that they may not have considered before. Failure can provide valuable feedback that helps individuals refine their strategies and improve their performance in future endeavors.

Furthermore, by embracing failure, individuals can develop resilience and a growth mindset. They learn to persevere in the face of setbacks and to view challenges as opportunities for growth and development. This mindset can help individuals bounce back from failures more quickly and move forward with renewed determination and a stronger sense of purpose. In the end, embracing failure can lead to greater success and fulfillment in both personal and professional life.

Section 3: Strategies for Taking Action and Embracing Failure

Overcoming the fear of failure and taking action toward goals requires a shift in mindset and the adoption of new strategies and habits. Here are some strategies that can help individuals overcome their fear of failure and take action toward their goals:

1. **Reframe failure:** Rather than seeing failure as a negative experience, reframe it as an opportunity for growth and learning. Embrace the idea that failure is a natural part of the process and can provide valuable feedback for improvement.
2. **Start small:** Taking small, incremental steps towards a goal can help build momentum and confidence. Set achievable goals and break them down into smaller tasks to make them more manageable.
3. **Visualize success:** Visualize yourself achieving your goal and the positive outcomes that will come from it. This can help build motivation and confidence in taking action.
4. **Build a support system:** Surround yourself with people who support and encourage you. Seek out mentors or accountability partners who can provide guidance and feedback.
5. **Take calculated risks:** Evaluate the potential risks and benefits of a decision, and take calculated risks rather than avoiding them altogether. This can help build confidence and lead to greater success.
6. **Practice self-compassion:** Be kind to yourself and acknowledge that setbacks and failures are a normal part of the process. Practice self-compassion and avoid negative self-talk.

By adopting these strategies and practicing them regularly, individuals can overcome their fear of failure and take action toward their goals with greater confidence and determination.

The importance of self-reflection and learning from failures

Self-reflection and learning from failures are crucial elements in achieving success. Failure provides an opportunity to learn from mistakes and improve oneself. By reflecting on what went wrong and what could have been done differently, individuals can gain valuable insights and grow from the experience.

Self-reflection allows individuals to assess their strengths and weaknesses, identify areas for improvement, and set new goals. It helps individuals to understand their values, beliefs, and motivations, which can be used to guide future actions and decision-making.

Learning from failures also helps individuals develop resilience and persistence. By facing and overcoming obstacles, individuals can build their confidence and develop a growth mindset. They can learn to view challenges as opportunities for growth and use their failures as stepping stones toward success.

Furthermore, self-reflection and learning from failures can also lead to new opportunities and ideas. By identifying areas for improvement and learning from mistakes, individuals can develop new strategies and approaches that can lead to even greater success.

Self-reflection and learning from failures are important in achieving success. They allow individuals to assess their strengths and weaknesses, develop resilience and persistence, and identify new opportunities for growth and success.

Taking action toward one's goals can lead to personal and professional growth, as it helps individuals to build confidence, gain experience, and develop new skills. Embracing failure is also important as it allows individuals to learn from their mistakes and use those lessons to make improvements and move forward. Successful individuals often experience failure multiple times before achieving success, and by reframing failure as an opportunity for growth, individuals can overcome their fear of failure and take action toward their goals. Self-reflection and learning from failures is also crucial in the process of growth and success. Therefore, you should take action toward their goals, embrace failure, and use self-reflection as a tool to learn from their experiences and make improvements in their journey toward success.

I hope you have found the previous chapters of this book informative and inspiring. Now, it's time to put the lessons you have learned into action. It's time to set your goals and take action toward achieving them. Remember, taking action is crucial in achieving personal and professional growth. It may not always be easy, but taking action is a necessary step toward success.

It's also important to remember that failure is not the end. Failure is an opportunity to learn and grow, and it's important to embrace it as a necessary step toward success. Successful individuals have experienced failure multiple times before achieving their goals, and by reframing failure as a chance for growth, you can overcome your fear of failure and take action toward your goals.

So, take the first step towards your goals, and don't be afraid to fail. Embrace your failures, learn from them, and keep moving forward. Remember to take time for self-reflection and make adjustments along the way. With persistence, resilience, and a growth mindset, you can achieve anything you set your mind to.

Chapter 12: The Value of Mentors and Networking

Success is not a solo journey. While individual effort, resilience, and persistence are critical to achieving one's goals, having the right support system can make all the difference. Mentors and networking play a pivotal role in the journey toward success, providing guidance, support, and access to resources that can help individuals overcome obstacles and reach their full potential.

In this chapter, we will explore the value of mentors and networking in the pursuit of success. We will discuss the benefits of having a mentor, the different types of mentors, and how to find one that aligns with your goals and values. We will also delve into the art of networking, highlighting its importance in building relationships, creating opportunities, and expanding one's knowledge and influence.

Through inspiring stories and practical tips, this chapter aims to empower you to leverage the power of mentors and networking to achieve their dreams and create a meaningful impact in their personal and professional lives.

Section 1: The Importance of Mentors

A mentor is a person who has more experience or knowledge in a particular area and provides guidance and support to someone who is less experienced. Mentors can be invaluable in helping us navigate the challenges of life and career, offering insights, advice, and a sounding board for our ideas and concerns.

In this section, we will discuss the benefits of having a mentor, how to find one, and what to look for in a good mentor. Whether you are just starting out in your career or looking to take it to the next level, a mentor can be a valuable asset in helping you achieve your goals.

The Role of a Mentor in personal and professional growth

A mentor can play a significant role in an individual's personal and professional growth. A mentor is someone who has more experience and knowledge than the mentee and is willing to share their insights, advice, and guidance to help the mentee develop their skills and reach their goals.

A mentor can provide a sounding board for ideas, offer feedback and constructive criticism, and serve as a source of inspiration and motivation. Mentors can help mentees navigate difficult situations, avoid common pitfalls, and provide opportunities for personal and professional growth.

The importance of having a mentor cannot be overstated, as it can make a significant difference in an individual's career trajectory and overall success.

How to find a mentor who aligns with our goals and values

Finding a mentor who aligns with our goals and values can be a challenging task, but it is an important step in personal and professional growth. Here are some tips for finding a mentor:

1. Identify your goals: Before you begin your search for a mentor, it's important to identify your goals and what you hope to achieve through mentorship. This will help you narrow down your search and find a mentor who aligns with your specific goals.

2. Look within your network: Start by looking within your existing network for potential mentors. This could be someone you already know or someone you've met through networking events or professional organizations.

3. Reach out to industry associations: Many industry associations have mentorship programs or can connect you with potential mentors in your field.

4. Attend events: Attend networking events, conferences, and workshops to meet people in your field who may be able to serve as a mentor.

5. Utilize online resources: There are many online mentorship platforms that can connect you with potential mentors, such as LinkedIn, SCORE, and MicroMentor.

6. Be proactive: Don't be afraid to reach out to someone you admire and ask them to be your mentor. Be clear about your goals and how they can help you achieve them.

Remember, mentorship is a two-way street. It's important to show your mentor that you are committed to your personal and professional growth and are willing to put in the work to achieve your goals.

The benefits of having a diverse group of mentors from various fields

Having a diverse group of mentors from various fields can offer several benefits for personal and professional growth. Firstly, it provides a broader perspective on different industries and fields. By seeking guidance from mentors in diverse fields, individuals can gain valuable insights into different approaches to problem-solving and decision-making. This exposure can help individuals develop a more well-rounded and innovative mindset.

Secondly, having mentors from various backgrounds can provide access to new networks and opportunities. As mentors come from different fields, they can introduce their mentees to their own network of contacts, providing them with valuable connections for future career opportunities or collaborations. Moreover, having a diverse group of mentors can help individuals build a more robust professional network, providing them with access to a broader range of industry contacts.

Thirdly, mentors from different fields can provide unique perspectives and insights that may not be available within one's industry or field. This cross-pollination of ideas and knowledge can lead to innovative thinking and creative problem-solving, which can be valuable in any profession.

Overall, having a diverse group of mentors can provide individuals with a wealth of knowledge and experience, enabling them to broaden their horizons and develop a more well-rounded approach to personal and professional growth.

Section 2: The Value of Networking

In today's fast-paced world, networking has become an essential skill for personal and professional growth. Whether you are an entrepreneur, a student, or a working professional, building a strong network can help you in numerous ways, from finding new opportunities to learning from others' experiences. In this section, we will explore the value of networking and how it can help you achieve your goals and aspirations. We will discuss the benefits of networking, strategies for building and maintaining a strong network, and how to effectively leverage your network to advance your career or business.

The benefits of networking for personal and professional growth

Networking refers to the process of building and maintaining relationships with people who can offer support, guidance, and opportunities for growth. The benefits of networking are numerous, both in personal and professional settings.

Firstly, networking provides access to new information, ideas, and perspectives. It allows individuals to learn from others in different fields or industries and gain insights into their own work. This exchange of knowledge and expertise can lead to new collaborations, partnerships, and business opportunities.

Secondly, networking helps to build a professional reputation and establish credibility within a particular field or industry. Meeting and connecting with influential people can help to enhance one's visibility and recognition in the industry, leading to potential job offers, promotions, and other opportunities for advancement.

Networking also provides emotional support and encouragement. It allows individuals to connect with others who share similar experiences and challenges, providing a sense of community and belonging. Additionally, networking can lead to the formation of mentorship relationships, where more experienced professionals provide guidance and advice to those who are newer to the industry.

Here are some strategies for effective networking:

Attend events: Attend networking events, conferences, and seminars to meet new people, build relationships, and expand your professional network. Be prepared with a clear elevator pitch and business cards.

Volunteer: Volunteer for industry-related events or charities to meet like-minded individuals and showcase your skills and expertise.

Utilize social media: Leverage social media platforms like LinkedIn, Twitter, and Instagram to connect with professionals in your field, join relevant groups, and share your knowledge and expertise.

Follow up: After meeting someone new, be sure to follow up with a personalized email or message, expressing your interest in continuing the conversation and exploring potential opportunities for collaboration.

Maintain relationships: Stay in touch with your network by regularly reaching out, sharing updates, and offering your assistance. Remember, networking is not just about making connections, but also about nurturing and maintaining them.

Building and maintaining professional relationships with authenticity and integrity

Building and maintaining professional relationships with authenticity and integrity is crucial in networking. It is essential to be genuine and transparent in all interactions and to build trust by being consistent and reliable. It is also important to communicate clearly and respectfully, as well as to listen actively to others.

Another aspect of maintaining professional relationships with authenticity and integrity is being mindful of giving back to your network. It is important to offer help or support when you can, and not just when you need something. This creates a mutually beneficial relationship and helps to strengthen connections in the long term.

Ultimately, building and maintaining professional relationships with authenticity and integrity requires a genuine interest in others and a commitment to building lasting connections. It is not just about getting ahead in one's career, but about building a supportive network that can provide guidance, inspiration, and opportunities for growth.

Section 3: Balancing Mentorship and Networking

Balancing Mentorship and Networking is crucial for achieving success in both personal and professional growth. While having a mentor can provide invaluable guidance and support, networking can open doors to new opportunities and connections. However, it's important to strike a balance between the two, as relying too heavily on one can limit the benefits of the other. In this chapter, we will explore how to effectively balance mentorship and networking to maximize their benefits and enhance our personal and professional growth.

Balancing mentorship and networking is important for achieving personal and professional growth. While having a mentor can provide valuable guidance and support, expanding our professional network through networking can lead to new opportunities and connections. However, it is important to find a balance between the two and not solely rely on one over the other.

Strategies for balancing mentorship and networking include being intentional about the relationships we cultivate, actively seeking out networking opportunities that align with our goals, and finding ways to incorporate the advice and guidance of mentors into our networking efforts. By finding a balance between mentorship and networking, we can enhance our personal and professional growth and achieve success in our endeavors.

How to leverage both mentorship and networking to achieve our goals and grow professionally

To leverage both mentorship and networking for professional growth, individuals should aim to strike a balance between building strong relationships with mentors and expanding their network of contacts. A mentor can offer guidance and advice based on their personal experiences, while a diverse network can provide new opportunities, fresh perspectives, and potential collaborators.

One way to balance mentorship and networking is to attend industry events and conferences, where individuals can meet new people and connect with potential mentors. Additionally, seeking out informational interviews with professionals in one's desired field can provide valuable insight and advice, as well as potentially lead to future opportunities.

It's also important to remember that mentorship and networking are not mutually exclusive - individuals can often find mentors through their network and expand their network through their mentorship relationships. By being open to both mentorship and networking opportunities, individuals can develop a well-rounded support system to help them achieve their goals and continue growing professionally.

In conclusion, having mentors and building a professional network are key components to achieving success in any field. Through mentorship, we gain valuable guidance and support, while networking allows us to build strong relationships and access new opportunities. Finding the right balance between these two can be challenging but is ultimately rewarding. By leveraging both mentorship and networking, we can grow both personally and professionally, and contribute to the success of those around us.

Part 4: Building a Success Mindset for Life

Chapter 13: Creating a Success Mindset for Personal Growth

In this chapter, we will explore the importance of creating a success mindset for personal growth. Our mindset plays a critical role in shaping our beliefs, attitudes, and behaviors, which in turn influence our success and happiness in life.

Developing a success mindset involves cultivating a positive and growth-oriented perspective, embracing challenges and failures as opportunities for learning and growth, setting and pursuing meaningful goals, and nurturing a resilient and adaptable mindset. By developing a success mindset, we can overcome obstacles, tap into our full potential, and live fulfilling and meaningful life.

We will discuss practical strategies for creating a successful mindset and overcoming limiting beliefs and negative self-talk. Let's begin our journey toward personal growth and success with an open and curious mind.

The Power of Positive Thinking

The power of positive thinking is a concept that has gained significant attention in recent years, particularly in the world of personal growth and development. The idea is that by maintaining a positive mindset and focusing on optimistic outcomes, individuals can achieve greater success in all areas of their lives, from relationships to career goals. This chapter will explore the benefits of positive thinking, strategies for cultivating a positive mindset, and ways in which positive thinking can lead to personal growth and success.

The impact of negativity on our mindset and personal growth

Negativity can have a significant impact on our mindset and personal growth. When we approach challenges or situations with a negative mindset, we limit our ability to see opportunities and solutions. Negative thinking can lead to self-doubt, fear, and a lack of confidence, which can prevent us from taking risks or pursuing our goals. This can result in missed opportunities and a lack of personal growth.

On the other hand, a positive mindset can help us to see opportunities, embrace challenges, and approach situations with confidence and determination. It can lead to increased resilience, a greater willingness to take risks, and ultimately, greater personal growth and success.

Techniques for Developing a positive mindset

Here are some techniques for developing a positive mindset:

Practice gratitude: Take time each day to reflect on what you are grateful for. Focusing on the positive aspects of your life can help shift your mindset to a more positive one.

Reframe negative thoughts: When you notice negative thoughts creeping in, challenge them and try to reframe them in a more positive way. For example, if you catch yourself thinking "I'm never going to succeed," reframe it as "I may face obstacles, but I am capable of overcoming them and achieving my goals."

Surround yourself with positivity: Seek out people who inspire and motivate you, and try to limit your exposure to negative influences. Fill your life with uplifting activities and experiences.

Practice mindfulness: Mindfulness techniques, such as meditation and deep breathing exercises, can help you focus on the present moment and reduce stress and anxiety.

Set realistic goals: Setting achievable goals and working towards them can help build confidence and a sense of accomplishment, which can contribute to a more positive mindset.

Take care of your physical health: Exercise regularly, eats a balanced diet, and get enough sleep. A healthy body can contribute to a healthy mind and a more positive outlook on life.

A positive mindset helps individuals to handle setbacks and challenges with greater ease and optimism, allowing them to bounce back quickly and learn from their experiences.

People with a positive mindset tend to be more optimistic, open-minded, and approachable, which can help them build and maintain positive relationships with others. It can also boost an individual's self-confidence, enabling them to take risks, face new challenges, and pursue their goals with greater determination.

Not only that but it helps to foster a growth mindset, where individuals are more likely to embrace new ideas and approaches, leading to greater creativity and innovation. Studies have shown that individuals with a positive mindset tend to have lower levels of stress, greater emotional resilience, and improved overall health.

Developing Self-Confidence and Self-Efficacy

Developing self-confidence and self-efficacy are crucial components of creating a success mindset for personal growth. Self-confidence refers to the belief in one's abilities and qualities, while self-efficacy refers to the belief in one's ability to achieve specific goals and tasks. Both are important for building resilience and taking action toward our goals.

To develop self-confidence, it is important to identify and focus on our strengths rather than weaknesses. We can also practice self-compassion and self-care to boost our self-esteem. Setting achievable goals and working towards them can also help build confidence as we see ourselves making progress.

To develop self-efficacy, it is important to break down larger goals into smaller, achievable tasks. This helps to build momentum and a sense of accomplishment. We can also seek out feedback from others and learn from our mistakes to improve our skills and abilities.

Both self-confidence and self-efficacy can be developed through practice and effort and can lead to increased motivation, productivity, and success in personal and professional endeavors.

Here are some strategies for building self-confidence and self-efficacy:

1. Set realistic goals: Setting small, achievable goals and achieving them can help boost your self-confidence and self-efficacy.

2. Focus on strengths: Focus on your strengths and positive attributes instead of your weaknesses. This can help increase your self-confidence.

3. Practice self-care: Taking care of yourself physically and emotionally can help boost your confidence and self-efficacy. This can include getting enough sleep, eating a healthy diet, and exercising regularly.

4. Learn new skills: Learning new skills can help you develop a sense of competence and increase your self-efficacy.

5. Embrace failure: Embrace failure as a necessary part of the learning process and use it as an opportunity to grow and improve.

6. Surround yourself with supportive people: Surround yourself with people who support and encourage you. This can help build your self-confidence and self-efficacy.

7. Visualize success: Visualize yourself succeeding in your goals and focus on the positive outcomes. This can help increase your self-confidence and self-efficacy.

The benefits of self-confidence and self-efficacy in achieving personal growth

Self-confidence and self-efficacy play a vital role in achieving personal growth. With high levels of self-confidence and self-efficacy, individuals are more likely to take risks, pursue their goals with determination, and persist through obstacles. They are also more likely to bounce back from failures, see setbacks as learning opportunities, and maintain a positive outlook.

Furthermore, individuals with high levels of self-confidence and self-efficacy tend to have a greater sense of self-worth, which can lead to more fulfilling relationships, better mental health, and an overall greater sense of well-being.

Ultimately, developing self-confidence and self-efficacy can lead to a more fulfilling and successful life, both personally and professionally.

Cultivating a Growth Mindset

Cultivating a growth mindset is essential in achieving personal growth. A growth mindset is a belief that one's abilities and intelligence can be developed through dedication and hard work. In contrast, a fixed mindset is the belief that one's abilities and intelligence are static traits that cannot be changed.

By cultivating a growth mindset, individuals are more likely to embrace challenges, persist in the face of obstacles, and see failures as opportunities for growth. They are also more likely to seek out new opportunities for learning and development, leading to increased personal and professional growth.

Strategies for cultivating a growth mindset include reframing negative self-talk, embracing challenges and failures as opportunities for growth, seeking out new learning opportunities, and surrounding oneself with positive and supportive individuals. By focusing on personal development and growth, individuals can achieve their goals and unlock their full potential.

Here are some strategies for developing a growth mindset:

1. Embrace challenges: Challenges provide an opportunity for growth and learning. Instead of shying away from challenges, embrace them as a chance to learn and improve.

2. View mistakes as learning opportunities: Instead of being discouraged by mistakes, view them as opportunities to learn and improve. Reflect on what went wrong and what you can do differently in the future.

3. Focus on effort over outcome: Instead of solely focusing on the end result, focus on the effort and progress made along the way. Celebrate small wins and milestones.

4. Learn from criticism: Instead of being defensive, listen to feedback and criticism with an open mind. Use it as an opportunity to learn and grow.

5. Surround yourself with supportive people: Surround yourself with people who believe in you and your abilities. Seek out mentors and friends who will support and encourage your growth.

6. Cultivate a love of learning: Adopt a mindset of continuous learning and growth. Seek new experiences and opportunities to expand your knowledge and skills.

By implementing these strategies, individuals can develop a growth mindset and reap the benefits of personal growth and success.

In conclusion, developing a success mindset is crucial for personal growth and achieving success in all areas of life. By harnessing the power of positive thinking, building self-confidence and self-efficacy, and cultivating a growth mindset, individuals can overcome challenges, embrace opportunities for growth, and achieve their goals. It's essential to understand the impact of negativity on our mindset and personal growth and to develop strategies for building a positive outlook on life.

Moreover, creating a success mindset requires dedication, perseverance, and a willingness to embrace failure as a necessary step toward growth. With the right mindset, anything is possible, and individuals can reach their full potential and live a fulfilling life. I encourage all you to take steps towards cultivating a success mindset and embracing the journey toward personal growth and success.

Chapter 14: Cultivating a Success Mindset in Relationships

Success is not just about individual achievement or financial gain. Our relationships with others play a crucial role in our personal growth and happiness. However, building strong and healthy relationships is not always easy. It requires us to develop a success mindset that enables us to communicate effectively, empathize with others, and navigate conflicts with grace and maturity.

In this chapter, we will explore the importance of cultivating a success mindset in our relationships. We will discuss the impact of our mindset on our interactions with others, and provide strategies for building positive and meaningful relationships that can support our personal growth and success. Whether you are seeking to improve your romantic relationships, build stronger friendships, or enhance your professional network, this chapter will provide you with valuable insights and practical tools for cultivating a successful mindset in your relationships.

The importance of mindset in relationships

The mindset we bring to our relationships can greatly impact their success and longevity. If we approach relationships with a negative or fixed mindset, we may struggle to communicate effectively, resolve conflicts, and maintain a healthy and fulfilling connection. However, when we cultivate a success mindset in our relationships, we are more likely to approach them with openness, empathy, and a willingness to learn and grow. This can lead to deeper and more satisfying connections with the important people in our lives.

The impact of negative thinking on relationships

Negative thinking can have a significant impact on relationships. It can lead to misunderstandings, miscommunications, and unnecessary conflict. Negative thoughts can make individuals defensive, closed-minded, and resistant to change or compromise. This can result in a breakdown of trust, mutual respect, and intimacy in relationships.

Additionally, negative thoughts can cause individuals to project their own insecurities and fears onto others, leading to further tension and strain in relationships. Overall, a negative mindset can undermine the health and success of relationships.

In relationships, different types of mindsets can impact the quality and longevity of the relationship. These mindsets can be either positive or negative and can shape how we approach our interactions with our partners. Some of the most common mindsets that can impact relationships include fixed mindsets, growth mindsets, scarcity mindsets, abundance mindsets, and victim mindsets.

Understanding our mindset in relationships is critical because it helps us identify the patterns and beliefs that shape our behavior and impact our interactions with our partners. By becoming aware of our mindset, we can develop a more positive and constructive approach to our relationships, leading to greater success and satisfaction in our personal lives.

The role of beliefs and values in shaping our mindset

Our beliefs and values play a significant role in shaping our mindset in relationships. Beliefs are the thoughts and convictions we have about ourselves, others, and the world around us, while values are the principles and standards that guide our behavior and decisions. Our beliefs and values can influence the way we approach relationships, the expectations we have of ourselves and others, and how we communicate and interact with others.

For instance, if we hold the belief that all relationships are bound to fail, we may be less likely to invest time and effort in building strong and healthy relationships. Similarly, if we value honesty and trust, we are more likely to prioritize communication and openness in our relationships. Understanding our beliefs and values can help us identify and shift any negative or limiting mindsets that may be impacting our relationships.

Strategies for identifying and challenging negative thoughts and beliefs

Strategies for identifying and challenging negative thoughts and beliefs in relationships include:

Practicing mindfulness: Mindfulness is the practice of being present and fully engaged in the current moment. It can help you become more aware of your thoughts and emotions, and allow you to challenge negative thoughts as they arise.

Reframing negative thoughts: Reframing involves looking at a situation from a different perspective. For example, instead of thinking "My partner never helps with the housework," you could reframe it as "My partner is busy with work right now, but they always help out when they have time."

Practicing self-compassion: Self-compassion involves treating yourself with kindness, care, and understanding. It can help you challenge negative self-talk and beliefs, and develop a more positive and supportive mindset.

Seeking support from a therapist or counselor: A therapist or counselor can help you identify and challenge negative thoughts and beliefs, and provide you with tools and strategies for developing a more positive mindset in relationships.

Practicing gratitude: Focusing on the positive aspects of your relationship and expressing gratitude for them can help you cultivate a more positive mindset and strengthen your connection with your partner.

Techniques for developing a positive mindset in relationships

Developing a positive mindset in relationships can be a powerful tool for personal growth and success. Here are some techniques for cultivating a positive mindset:

Practice gratitude: Focus on what you appreciate about your partner and your relationship, rather than what you don't like. Make a habit of expressing gratitude and appreciation regularly.

Reframe negative thoughts: Challenge negative thoughts and try to see things from a different perspective. For example, instead of thinking "my partner never listens to me," reframe it as "my partner may not always understand me, but they try their best."

Communicate effectively: Practice active listening, and be clear and direct in your communication. Focus on finding solutions instead of blaming each other.

Practice forgiveness: Let go of grudges and resentments, and practice forgiveness. Holding onto negative emotions can harm your relationship.

Focus on strengths: Recognize each other's strengths and work together to build on them. Encourage and support each other in pursuing goals and aspirations.

By practicing these techniques, you can develop a positive mindset in your relationships, which can lead to greater personal growth and success.

The role of mindset in managing conflicts and challenges in relationships

Our mindset plays a critical role in managing conflicts and challenges in relationships. It determines how we perceive, interpret, and respond to difficult situations. A positive and growth-oriented mindset can help us approach conflicts with a constructive and solution-focused attitude, while a negative mindset can lead to defensiveness, blame, and escalation of conflicts.

Our mindset can also impact how we handle setbacks and failures in relationships, either by learning from them and moving forward or getting stuck in a cycle of resentment and blame. Therefore, developing a success mindset in relationships can help us build healthier and more fulfilling connections with others.

Supporting Others in Their Success

Supporting others in their success has numerous benefits. First, it creates a positive and uplifting environment where everyone feels valued and supported. It fosters a culture of collaboration and teamwork, which can lead to increased productivity and success for all individuals involved.

Additionally, supporting others in their success can help to build stronger and more meaningful relationships, as it demonstrates a willingness to help others achieve their goals and aspirations. It can also lead to personal growth, as helping others can be a source of fulfillment and purpose. Finally, supporting others in their success can create a ripple effect, as individuals who feel supported are more likely to pass on the same level of support and encouragement to others.

Here are some strategies for cultivating a success mindset in

relationships through support and encouragement:

Celebrate their achievements: When someone achieves something great, celebrate it with them. Let them know how proud you are of their hard work and dedication.

Offer encouragement: Be there to offer words of encouragement when they need it most. Let them know that you believe in them and their abilities.

Listen actively: When someone is going through a difficult time or facing a challenge, actively listen to them. Offer support and guidance where needed, but also allow them to work through their emotions and thoughts.

Provide resources: If someone is working towards a goal or project, offer your resources and connections to help them succeed. Whether it's lending a hand or connecting them with someone who can help, your support can make all the difference.

Be a sounding board: Sometimes, all someone needs is a listening ear. Be there to listen to their ideas, concerns, and thoughts. Offer feedback where appropriate, but also allow them the space to come to their own conclusions.

By offering support and encouragement, you can cultivate a success mindset in your relationships and help those around you achieve their goals and aspirations.

In conclusion, cultivating a successful mindset in our relationships can have a profound impact on our personal and professional growth. By understanding the different types of mindsets that can impact relationships, challenging negative thoughts and beliefs, and developing positive thinking patterns, we can build stronger and more fulfilling relationships.

Additionally, by supporting and encouraging others in their success, we can foster a culture of growth and achievement in our personal and professional networks. It is essential to recognize that mindset is not just about achieving financial success, but also about developing meaningful relationships and personal growth. By taking steps to cultivate a success mindset in our relationships, we can lead more fulfilling lives and contribute to the success of those around us.

Therefore, I encourage you to reflect on their mindset in relationships, identify any negative patterns, and work towards developing a positive and supportive mindset. By doing so, we can create stronger, more fulfilling relationships and contribute to the success of those around us.

Chapter 15: Achieving Success in Business and Career

A positive mindset is essential for achieving success in business and career because it influences the way you approach challenges and opportunities. Having a positive mindset means that you view obstacles and setbacks as opportunities for growth and learning, rather than as roadblocks to success.

As we have discussed before as well, Here are some reasons why a positive mindset is important for achieving success in business and career:

- A positive mindset helps you stay resilient in the face of challenges and setbacks. Instead of giving up or getting discouraged, you're more likely to persist and find a way forward.

- A positive mindset can help you think more creatively and come up with innovative solutions to problems. By focusing on what's possible instead of what's impossible, you're more likely to find new and effective ways of achieving your goals.

- A positive mindset can also help you stay motivated and focused on your goals. When you believe in yourself and your abilities, you're more likely to take action and stay committed to your goals, even when the going gets tough.

- A positive mindset can also help you build stronger relationships with others. By approaching others with positivity and optimism, you're more likely to build trust and rapport, which can be invaluable in business and career.

- Also, a positive mindset is good for your overall health and well-being. Studies have shown that people with positive mindsets are less stressed, have better immune systems, and live longer, healthier lives.

Having a positive mindset is crucial for achieving success in business and career. It helps you stay resilient, creative, motivated, and focused on your goals, while also improving your relationships and overall well-being.

Defining Success in Business and Career

Defining success in business and career is a deeply personal process that requires a growth mindset. A growth mindset is a belief that your abilities and intelligence can be developed through hard work, dedication, and learning from failures. When you approach success with a growth mindset, you're more likely to focus on the process of growth and development, rather than just the end result.

Understanding what success means to you is an important step in defining success in business and career. Success can mean different things to different people, depending on their values, goals, and priorities. For some, success may mean achieving financial freedom, while for others it may mean making a positive impact in the world or finding personal fulfillment in their work.

Here are some ways to approach defining success in business and career through a growth mindset point of view:

1. **Reflect on your values:** Start by thinking about what's important to you in life. What are your core values and beliefs? How do these values align with your career goals? When you have a clear understanding of your values, it's easier to define what success means to you.

2. **Set meaningful goals:** Rather than focusing solely on financial or status-based goals, set goals that are meaningful and align with your values. What are the things that you want to achieve in your career that would make you feel fulfilled and satisfied?

3. **Embrace challenges and failures:** A growth mindset means embracing challenges and failures as opportunities for growth and learning. When you encounter setbacks or obstacles, try to see them as opportunities to learn and improve.

4. **Seek feedback:** Seeking feedback from others is an important part of a growth mindset. By seeking feedback, you can learn from others and identify areas for improvement.

5. **Focus on the journey:** Finally, when defining success in business and career, it's important to focus on the journey, not just the destination. Success is not just about achieving a specific goal, but also about the growth and development that happens along the way.

Defining success in business and career through a growth mindset means focusing on personal values, setting meaningful goals, embracing challenges and failures, seeking feedback, and focusing on the journey. By approaching success with a growth mindset, you can create a more fulfilling and meaningful career path.

The benefits of a growth mindset in business and career

Having a growth mindset can have numerous benefits for achieving success in business and career. Here are some of the key benefits:

1. **Increased Resilience:** People with a growth mindset are more resilient in the face of challenges and setbacks. They view failure as an opportunity to learn and grow, rather than as a reflection of their abilities. This resilience helps them bounce back from setbacks and stay motivated and focused on their goals.

2. **Improved Creativity and Innovation:** People with a growth mindset are more likely to think outside the box and come up with innovative solutions to problems. They are not limited by their current knowledge or abilities, and instead focus on developing new skills and expanding their knowledge base.

3. **Greater Adaptability:** People with a growth mindset are better able to adapt to changing circumstances in the business world. They are not afraid to try new approaches and pivot when necessary to achieve their goals.

4. **Increased Learning and Development:** People with a growth mindset are committed to continuous learning and development. They are open to feedback and constructive criticism and use it to improve their skills and abilities.

5. **Stronger Relationships:** People with a growth mindset tend to build stronger relationships with others in the business world. They are more open to collaborating and sharing ideas and are not threatened by others' success.

6. **Higher Levels of Achievement:** Ultimately, people with a growth mindset tend to achieve higher levels of success in business and careers. They are more likely to take risks, persist in the face of challenges, and continue to grow and develop their skills and abilities over time.

Therefore, having a growth mindset can provide numerous benefits for achieving success in business and career, including increased resilience, improved creativity and innovation, greater adaptability, increased learning and development, stronger relationships, and higher levels of achievement. By adopting a growth mindset, you can set yourself up for long-term success and fulfillment in your career.

Achieving success in business and career is not only about having the right technical skills and knowledge. It also requires the right mindset. A growth mindset can help you set meaningful goals, take action towards achieving them, learn from failures, build strong relationships, persevere through challenges, and adapt to change. Here's how each of these elements can help you achieve success:

Setting Goals: Having a growth mindset helps you set clear and achievable goals for your career. With a clear vision of what you want to achieve, you can break down your goals into smaller, more achievable steps, and stay motivated to reach them.

Taking Action: A growth mindset encourages you to take action towards your goals, even if you are uncertain about the outcome. You are not afraid of failure or setbacks, and see them as opportunities to learn and grow.

Learning from Failures: With a growth mindset, you can learn from your failures and setbacks. Rather than seeing them as a reflection of your abilities, you see them as opportunities to gain valuable insights and feedback that can help you improve.

Building Relationships: Building strong relationships is critical for success in business and career. A growth mindset helps you connect with others, understand their perspectives, and work collaboratively to achieve common goals.

Persevering through Challenges: Inevitably, you will face challenges and obstacles on your path to success. With a growth mindset, you are more likely to persevere through these challenges and remain focused on your goals.

Adapting to Change: The business world is constantly changing, and success requires the ability to adapt to new circumstances. With a growth mindset, you can embrace change as an opportunity for growth and find new ways to succeed in the face of uncertainty.

A growth mindset can help you achieve success in business and your career by enabling you to set meaningful goals, take action toward them, build strong relationships, persevere through challenges, and adapt to change. With the right mindset, you can create a path to success that is both fulfilling and sustainable.

Fostering Positive Habits for Business and Career Success

Fostering positive habits is an important part of achieving success in business and career. Habits are routines that we engage in regularly, often without conscious effort. When we cultivate positive habits, we set ourselves up for success by creating a consistent framework for achieving our goals. Here are some examples of positive habits that can lead to success:

1. Planning and Prioritizing: One habit that can help you achieve success in business and career is planning and prioritizing your tasks. By setting aside time each day or week to plan your goals and prioritize your tasks, you can ensure that you are working on the most important things first.

For example, a successful business executive might start each day by reviewing their schedule and prioritizing their tasks for the day based on their goals and deadlines. By planning ahead, they can avoid getting sidetracked by less important tasks and stay focused on achieving their objectives.

2. Time Management: Time management is another important habit for success in business and career. By managing your time effectively, you can ensure that you are making the most of your resources and avoiding burnout.

For example, a successful entrepreneur might use a time-tracking app to monitor their activities throughout the day, identifying areas where they can save time or delegate tasks to others. By being mindful of their time, they can ensure that they are working efficiently and making the most of their available resources.

3. Networking: Networking is a critical habit for success in business and career. By building relationships with others in your industry or profession, you can gain valuable insights, opportunities, and support.

For example, a successful sales executive might attend networking events regularly, meet new people and build relationships with potential clients or partners. By staying connected with others in their industry, they can stay up-to-date on new trends, opportunities, and challenges.

4. Continuous Learning: Continuous learning is another important habit for success in business and career. By seeking out new knowledge and skills, you can stay ahead of the curve and continue to grow and develop over time.

For example, a successful marketer might read industry publications, attend conferences, or take online courses to stay up-to-date on new trends and best practices. By continuously learning and evolving, they can maintain a competitive edge and stay relevant in a rapidly changing field.

Therefore, fostering positive habits is an important part of achieving success in business and career. By planning and prioritizing your tasks, managing your time effectively, networking with others, and continuously learning, you can set yourself up for long-term success and fulfillment in your professional life.

The Role of Habits in achieving success

Habits play a crucial role in achieving success in business and career. Habits are deeply ingrained patterns of behavior that we engage in regularly, often without conscious effort. They can be either positive or negative, and they have a powerful impact on our daily routines, productivity, and overall success.

Positive habits are those that contribute to our well-being and help us achieve our goals. Examples of positive habits include planning and prioritizing, managing our time effectively, networking with others, and continuously learning. By cultivating positive habits, we can create a framework for success that enables us to work towards our goals consistently over time.

Negative habits, on the other hand, can hold us back from achieving success. Examples of negative habits include procrastination, lack of focus, disorganization, and poor time management. These habits can lead to stress, burnout, and a lack of progress toward our goals.

The role of habits in achieving success is critical. Positive habits can contribute to consistency, productivity, focus, resilience, and self-improvement, all of which are essential for success in business and career. By cultivating positive habits and eliminating negative ones, we can create a framework for success that enables us to achieve our goals and fulfill our potential.

The importance of a strong support system in achieving success

A strong support system is essential for achieving success in any area of life, including business and career. A support system consists of people who provide emotional, professional, and practical support, and who help us to achieve our goals. Here are some reasons why a strong support system is important for achieving success:

Motivation: A strong support system can provide motivation and encouragement when we feel stuck or discouraged. When we are surrounded by people who believe in us and our goals, we are more likely to stay motivated and focused on our path to success.

Accountability: A support system can also provide accountability. When we share our goals and aspirations with others, we are more likely to follow through on our commitments. Our support system can hold us accountable for our actions, and provide feedback and guidance when needed.

Guidance: A strong support system can provide guidance and advice. When we face challenges or obstacles, our support system can offer insights and perspectives that we may not have considered. They can help us to navigate difficult situations, make informed decisions, and avoid costly mistakes.

Networking: A support system can also provide networking opportunities. By connecting with people in our industry or field, we can expand our knowledge, learn from other's experiences, and access new opportunities. Our support system can introduce us to new contacts, share information about job openings or industry trends, and provide recommendations and referrals.

Stress relief: Finally, a strong support system can provide stress relief. When we are under pressure or feeling overwhelmed, our support system can offer emotional support and practical help. They can help us to manage our workload, provide a listening ear, and offer encouragement when we need it most.

Therefore, a strong support system is essential for achieving success in business and career. It can provide motivation, accountability, guidance, networking opportunities, and stress relief. By building and nurturing a strong support system, we can increase our chances of achieving our goals, overcoming challenges, and reaching our full potential.

Strategies for achieving success while maintaining personal fulfillment and well-being

Achieving success in business and career is important, but it shouldn't come at the expense of our personal fulfillment and well-being.

To achieve success while maintaining balance and well-being, we need to prioritize self-care, set healthy boundaries, and stay connected to our values and purpose. This means taking breaks, practicing mindfulness, and engaging in activities that bring us joy and fulfillment. It also means setting boundaries around work, technology, and other stressors, and creating space for rest and relaxation.

Overall, It means staying connected to our values and purpose, and aligning our goals with our deeper sense of meaning and fulfillment. By prioritizing our well-being and fulfillment, we can achieve success in business and career while living a balanced and fulfilling life.

In conclusion, developing a growth mindset and positive habits is essential for achieving success in business and career. By embracing challenges, learning from failures, seeking feedback, persisting through obstacles, and fostering positive habits, we can develop the skills and mindset needed to achieve our goals.

Moreover, building a strong support system and prioritizing our personal fulfillment and well-being are crucial for maintaining balance and perspective in the pursuit of success. It's important to remember that success is a journey and that setbacks and challenges are opportunities for growth and learning.

As we pursue our own paths to success, let's stay committed to our goals, stay connected to our values and purpose, and stay open to the opportunities and possibilities that lie ahead. With the right mindset and habits, and the support of our community, we can achieve success and live a fulfilling and meaningful life.

Chapter 16: Building a Legacy of Success

While financial success is an important aspect of achieving our goals, it is not the only measure of success. Building a legacy of success that goes beyond the financial gain is important for leaving a positive impact on the world and creating a lasting legacy. Legacy building is about creating something that will live beyond our years, something that will be remembered for generations to come.

It is about creating a sense of purpose and meaning that goes beyond our own personal gains. A legacy of success can be built in many ways, whether it be through philanthropy, entrepreneurship, mentorship, or any other means of positively impacting the world around us. By building a legacy of success, we can make a difference in the lives of others and leave a lasting impact that extends far beyond our own lifetime.

Building a legacy of success can inspire and motivate others to do the same. When we create something that positively impacts the world, we can inspire others to do the same and create a ripple effect of positive change. By building a legacy of success, we can become a positive influence on the world and leave a lasting impact that extends far beyond our own lifetime.

Identifying your values and purpose

Identifying your values and purpose is a crucial step in building a legacy of success beyond financial gain. Your values are the principles and beliefs that guide your decision-making and shape your worldview, while your purpose is your unique reason for being and the impact you want to make in the world. By understanding your values and purpose, you can align your actions with what truly matters to you and create a legacy that is meaningful and fulfilling.

To identify your values, take some time to reflect on what is important to you. What principles do you hold dear, and what beliefs do you want to live by? You may also look to your past experiences and relationships to identify what has been most meaningful to you.

To identify your purpose, consider what motivates and inspires you. What impact do you want to make in the world, and what unique gifts and talents do you have to offer? You may also think about what legacy you want to leave behind and what kind of impact you want to have on future generations.

Once you have identified your values and purpose, use them as a guide for your actions and decision-making. Align your goals and aspirations with what truly matters to you, and work towards creating a legacy that reflects your values and purpose. By doing so, you can build a legacy of success that extends far beyond financial gain and creates a lasting impact on the world.

Importance of aligning your legacy with your values and purpose

Aligning your legacy with your values and purpose is essential for creating a meaningful and fulfilling life. When your actions and goals are aligned with your values and purpose, you are more likely to feel a sense of fulfillment and happiness, and to create a legacy that is true to who you are.

One strategy for identifying your values and purpose is to **engage in self-reflection.** Take some time to think about what is most important to you and what brings you the most joy and fulfillment. Consider your past experiences and relationships, and think about what has been most meaningful to you. You may also find it helpful to journal or talk with a trusted friend or mentor to gain clarity on your values and purpose.

Another strategy is to **seek out experiences and opportunities** that align with your values and purpose. Look for ways to volunteer or get involved in causes that are important to you, or seek out jobs and career paths that align with your purpose and allow you to make an impact in the world. By taking action and engaging with the world around you, you can gain a better understanding of your values and purpose and find ways to align your legacy with them.

Therefore, , aligning your legacy with your values and purpose is key to creating a meaningful and fulfilling life. By engaging in self-reflection and seeking out experiences and opportunities that align with your values and purpose, you can identify your unique path to success and create a legacy that reflects who you are and what you stand for.

Planning to create your own legacy that glorifies your success

Planning for a legacy of success involves creating a vision for the impact you want to make on the world and setting goals and milestones to achieve that vision. Here are some strategies for planning your legacy of success:

Creating a vision for your legacy: Start by reflecting on what kind of impact you want to make through your business or career. Think about what kind of legacy you want to leave behind and what values and principles you want to uphold. This may involve considering your personal and professional goals, as well as the impact you want to have on your industry or society as a whole.

Setting goals and milestones: Once you have a vision for your legacy of success, break it down into smaller, achievable goals and milestones. Consider what steps you need to take to achieve your vision, and set measurable goals that will help you get there. This may involve creating a timeline or action plan and seeking out resources or support to help you achieve your goals.

Examples of goals and milestones for building a legacy of success may include:

- Developing a product or service that solves a pressing problem in your industry or community
- Building a company culture that promotes ethical and sustainable practices
- Becoming a thought leader or influencer in your field through speaking engagements or publications
- Mentoring or supporting the growth of future leaders in your industry
- Creating a positive impact on society through philanthropy or advocacy efforts

Therefore, planning for a legacy of success involves creating a clear vision for the impact you want to make through your business or career, and setting goals and milestones to achieve that vision. By breaking down your legacy into smaller, achievable steps, you can take concrete actions toward creating a meaningful and lasting impact on your industry, community, and society.

Taking action to build your legacy

Taking action to build your legacy involves intentionally cultivating a professional brand, giving back to your community, mentoring and empowering others, and creating a culture of excellence.

These strategies can help you create a lasting impact and build a legacy of success that goes beyond financial gain.

Building a professional brand: Your professional brand is the way you present yourself to the world, and it can have a significant impact on your success and legacy. This involves creating a consistent image that reflects your values, skills, and expertise. This may involve developing a strong online presence, creating content that demonstrates your thought leadership, and networking with others in your industry.

Giving back to your community: Building a legacy of success involves making a positive impact on the world around you. Giving back to your community can take many forms, such as volunteering, donating to charity, or supporting local businesses. By investing in the people and organizations around you, you can create a ripple effect of positive change.

Mentoring and empowering others: A key part of building a legacy of success is empowering others to achieve their own goals and make their own impact. This may involve mentoring younger professionals, sharing your expertise with others in your field, or creating opportunities for others to develop their skills and leadership potential.

Creating a culture of excellence: Building a culture of excellence involves setting high standards for yourself and those around you, and creating an environment that supports growth and innovation. This may involve promoting transparency, accountability, and collaboration within your organization or industry.

Examples of individuals who have built a successful legacy include:

1. Oprah Winfrey, who has built a media empire that promotes personal growth, empowerment, and philanthropy.

2. Bill Gates, who has used his wealth and influence to support global health initiatives and advance technological innovation.

3. Michelle Obama, who has used her platform to promote education, health and wellness, and women's rights.

Hence, taking action to build your legacy involves cultivating a professional brand, giving back to your community, mentoring and empowering others, and creating a culture of excellence. By following these strategies and looking to examples of successful legacy builders, you can create a lasting impact that goes beyond financial gain and inspires others to make their own mark on the world.

Reflection and continued growth

Reflection and continued growth are important components of building a successful legacy that goes beyond financial gain. Reflection involves taking the time to assess your progress, evaluate your strengths and weaknesses, and identify areas for improvement. This can help you stay on track with your goals and ensure that you are aligned with your values and purpose.

Continued growth involves committing to ongoing learning and development, and seeking out new opportunities for growth and expansion. This may involve attending workshops or conferences, pursuing further education or certification, or seeking out new challenges or experiences.

Reflection and continued growth can be facilitated through

various strategies, including:

Regular self-assessment: Set aside time to reflect on your progress, identify areas for improvement, and set new goals. This can help you stay on track with your vision and ensure that you are continuously improving and growing.

Seeking feedback: Seek out feedback from trusted colleagues, mentors, or advisors. This can help you gain a fresh perspective on your strengths and weaknesses, and identify areas for improvement.

Engaging in ongoing learning and development: Commit to ongoing learning and development by attending workshops, seminars, or conferences, pursuing further education or certification, or seeking out new challenges or experiences.

Surrounding yourself with supportive and challenging individuals: Surround yourself with individuals who are supportive of your goals and values, but who also challenge you to grow and improve.

Reflection and continued growth can help you build a legacy of success that is not just focused on financial gain, but also on personal and professional growth and development. By committing to ongoing learning and improvement, you can ensure that you are constantly evolving and expanding your impact, and leaving a lasting legacy that inspires and empowers others to do the same.

In conclusion, building a legacy of success that goes beyond financial gain requires a thoughtful and intentional approach. By aligning your legacy with your values and purpose, creating a vision for your legacy, setting goals and milestones, and taking action to build your professional brand and give back to your community, you can create a lasting impact that inspires and empowers others.

Reflection and continued growth are also critical components of building a successful legacy, as they allow you to stay aligned with your values and purpose, identify areas for improvement, and seek out new opportunities for growth and expansion.

Building a legacy of success is a journey that requires commitment, dedication, and hard work. But by staying focused on your vision and purpose, and by continuously learning and growing, you can build a legacy that transcends financial gain and leaves a lasting impact on the world.

Bonus Point: Being spiritual takes you a long way to having a great & healthy mindset.

Spirituality can play a significant role in bringing a healthy and positive mindset that leads to a happy life. Here are some ways in which spirituality can help:

1. Mindfulness and awareness: Spirituality encourages one to be mindful and aware of the present moment, which helps to reduce stress and anxiety. It enables individuals to focus on what is essential and not get distracted by external factors.

2. Gratitude: Spirituality helps individuals to cultivate gratitude and appreciate the simple things in life. It helps to shift the focus from what one does not have to what one has and fosters a sense of contentment and fulfillment.

3. Forgiveness: Spirituality teaches individuals the value of forgiveness and letting go of resentment and anger. It helps to release negative emotions and promotes a sense of inner peace and harmony.

4. Compassion and empathy: Spirituality encourages individuals to be compassionate and empathetic towards others. It helps to develop a sense of connection and community, which leads to a more fulfilling and satisfying life.

5. **Purpose and meaning:** Spirituality helps individuals to find purpose and meaning in life. It enables them to connect with their inner selves and discover their true calling, leading to a sense of fulfillment and happiness.

Spirituality can help you develop a healthy and positive mindset, leading to a more fulfilling and satisfying life. By cultivating mindfulness, gratitude, forgiveness, compassion, empathy, and purpose, individuals can find inner peace, happiness, and meaning in life.

Make Notes

It's a Wrap

Mindset matters when it comes to achieving success in life. Success is more than just accumulating wealth or achieving fame; it is about living a fulfilling and purposeful life that aligns with your values and beliefs. In this book, we have explored the power of mindset and the importance of cultivating a growth mindset in all areas of life, including personal relationships, health and wellness, business, and career. We have also discussed the critical role of habits, support systems, and planning for building a legacy of success that goes beyond financial gain.

To achieve true success, it is essential to develop a positive and growth-oriented mindset, embrace challenges, learn from failures, seek feedback, and persist through obstacles. It is also crucial to surround ourselves with a strong support system, cultivate positive habits, identify our values and purpose, and set goals and milestones for our personal and professional growth.

Through this book, I hope to have inspired you to take a holistic approach to success, one that prioritizes personal fulfillment and well-being as well as financial gain. With the right mindset and a commitment to growth and learning, anyone can achieve success and build a legacy that makes a meaningful impact on the world. Remember, mindset matters, and success is more than just money.

P.S: You can pass on this book to someone in need to have it and keep sharing & supporting a positive mindset so that no one gives ups on their dream and everyone lead a successful life & lifestyle.

Thank You!!